The Spotlight Operator's Handbook

by

June Abernathy

Spring Knoll Press
Johnson City, Tennessee 37601

Copyright and Liability

The Spotlight Operator's Handbook

Written by June Abernathy

Published by
Spring Knoll Press
Johnson City, Tennessee 37601
www.SpringKnollPress.com
Copyright © 2019 June Abernathy

ISBN: 978-1-7330064-0-8

Printed in the United States of America

Table of Contents

Chapter/Page

Chapter 1:
Introduction

Running a spotlight is harder than it looks. To do it well, you need to understand how the light and its controls work, you need some training, and you need some practice. Unfortunately, for many people, your first exposure to operating a spotlight is getting handed a pile of color and directions to the spot booth or catwalk one day when people are short, and maybe, if you're lucky, getting a quick rundown on the controls from someone in a hurry to get to their own place before the show starts.

A followspot is the ultimate "Intelligent Light". Unlike the robotic moving lights that the term usually implies, a followspot, with a good operator, is the only light that thinks. A good spotlight operator needs to be able to multi-task – working all the controls on the light, often simultaneously, while watching the target, listening to the show, and listening to whoever is calling cues for the spotlights. In most professional environments, a touring show is seen by the operator for the first time at showtime - paying audience in place, figuring it out (and having it called to you) as you go.

Spotlights are used in every aspect of the entertainment business – Theater, Dance, Opera, Concerts, Videos, Standup Comedy, and more. Different types of performances have different styles of lighting, and a followspot operator can end up in many types of environments. You might end up sitting on a rock and roll lighting truss, strapped into a tiny seat like a tail gunner with a small light between your knees, or you might be 300 feet away from an Opera stage in a wide glass booth operating a 3,000-watt Gladiator that is 8 feet long.

There are dozens of different brands and styles of spotlights, made for different applications and throw distances. Each one is different, in its way, but all of them have the same essential controls. Once you become familiar with a couple of different models, adapting to something new becomes pretty quick work.

I have not included specific information about running or maintaining Carbon Arc Spotlights in this manual. They are no longer manufactured and are rarely seen any more. I didn't feel that it was worth the space to address their specific issues.

This book is an attempt to give you the information that, in at least my opinion, every good spotlight operator should know. It isn't really a substitute for hands on training and experience, but it's a start.

Chapter 2:
Parts and Control

All spotlights are different. But most have the same essential controls – the knobs and levers that allow you to control the size, intensity, beam, and color of the light. All spots also have controls that allow you to regulate the freedom of movement that the light has and help level and balance the spot. These are the controls that you look for when you find yourself working an unfamiliar light.

The spotlight will either be sitting on a base or mounted on a pipe of some kind. Some spots are hung down from above. All will consist of the Spotlight Head – the actual luminaire – set into a Yoke, which swivels and has a pipe that either sets into a base on the floor or slides up into an overhead fitting. There is usually some way to adjust the height of the yoke. Whatever kind of base and yoke configuration you have, all of them will generally have a locking handle to lock down and release the Tilt – the up/down motion of the light, and another to lock and release the Pan – the side to side motion of the light. While you generally don't want these locked down unless you are moving the light, or holding it in position to work on it, depending on the way the light balances, you may not want to have them completely free and open for operation either. Sometimes, just a little drag is helpful, so the light doesn't wobble and sway the instant you touch it or react to your touch in too exaggerated a manner. It's worth playing with them to get the tension you want. Do this after you Balance the light for weight. (See Balance – Chapter 7).

All lights have some kind of focusing apparatus – a way to adjust the internal lenses for optimal size, sharpness, and brightness. Many have a couple of adjustments – one for rough focus, and another for fine focus. On a big light, the rough focus is accomplished with the Trombone. The Trombone (often referred to in manuals as the Spot Size Control Knob or something like that) is a handle that moves the front lens in relation to the others, changing the focus. This affects the size that you can achieve on stage, as well as the brightness possible, and, of course, the edge. The longer the focal length – that is, the farther forward you can set your Trombone, the smaller your beam will be. But also, the brighter your beam will be. So, usually, you want to set the Trombone so that you can achieve the largest size that you will need (a generous full body size, maybe a Two-shot – large enough to include two people), and no bigger. (Make sure your Iris is full wide open when you are doing this). This ensures that you will retain as much brightness as possible, and also, that you will be able to get as small as you need to – down to a head shot or pin spot size – when you close the iris as small as possible. The Trombone handle should have a locking mechanism to hold it in place once you have it to your desired position. Generally, you rotate the handle counterclockwise to unlock, clockwise to lock in place. Once you have your Trombone set, on a light equipped with a separate fine focus, you want to adjust that until you have a clean sharp edge on the light. There are shows and designs that want the spot to have a constant soft edge, and you can do this by fuzzing the fine focus. However, most designers prefer to use a diffusion gel to accomplish this effect, as it lets the light stay in proper focus and optimal brightness.

Most venues with permanent spot positions frown on individual operators moving the Trombone or adjusting the focus, as they have already got those set for optimal size and brightness. But there are some shows that require you to adjust the Trombone for a specific moment in the show (say, pulling back to cover a large group of people or a set piece). And, many spots have a weak or useless friction lock on the Trombone handle, meaning that it can slide back when the light is tipped up, or if the operator grabs it to use as a handle. For this reason, it is a really good idea to mark the Trombone position with a piece of tape, particularly if its "home" position is anything other than all the way forward. If you've got a loose one, it is often also a good idea to put a piece of tape vertically in back of (and maybe also in front of) the handle so it can't slide around during operation.

The main controls that you will use in running the light are the Chop, the Douser, and the Iris. These three controls are usually grouped together, somewhere in the middle of the light, to put them in the gate of the lamp's focus system. (The "gate" is the focal point of the lamp - the place where the reflector of the lamp forces the individual beams of light to converge. In a spotlight, this is the optimal place for placing controls to shape the light). On some lights, particularly smaller models, the handles for the controls are elsewhere – in the front or back of the lamp, for instance, although the internal controls are generally still in the gate. You want to reach a point where you can work these controls by touch, without needing to take your eyes off of the stage to look at your hands.

The Chop (also called the chopper, shutter, masking shutters, or shaping gate) is actually rarely used in modern theatrical design. Many operators tape or tie it off, so they will not grab it by mistake in the middle of a show. Traditionally, the Chop controls a pair of horizontal shutters that cut off the top and bottom of the light, squaring it off. You can use this control as you would in a Leko – to cut off of scenery or the proscenium or apron edge. But this really only works if the light is in a stationary position, and that is rarely the case with a followspot. Sometimes, in an emergency like a Light Board failure, for instance, they will ask the spots to "Strip and Cover" (sometimes called "Flood and Cover"). That is, open up as wide as you can to cover the whole stage. This means pulling the Trombone back to get large enough. Then, you use your Chopper to cut in to the top of the proscenium and bottom of the apron and lock your light in place. The Chop can be used to completely cut off the light. It's not a particularly attractive way to do it – it doesn't slowly dim the light the way the Douser will – but it can be used in a pinch, particularly if you have a loose or leaky Douser. Not all lights have a Chopper. Some lights have two – the traditional Horizontal Chop, and also a Vertical Chop, cutting in from the sides. This gives the fixture a full set of shutters, like a Leko. The Vertical Chop can occasionally be helpful, if, for instance, you have a character standing next to a proscenium wall or some other piece of scenery for an extended time like a monologue or a narration, and you want to cut off of it. Still, it's very rarely used in the theater.

The Douser is the control that is actually meant to dim and cut off the light. There are various types of dousers – vertical plates that close like a book, often with a jagged edge to soften the edge, horizontal plates that do much the same, iris type leaves that close like a camera shutter, and a variety of others. There are even electronic dousers that work with a slider control. The design doesn't really matter to you as an operator. What matters is that it moves easily from wide open and bright, dimming smoothly and evenly down to completely out. On most lights, you reach full brightness before the end of handle travel. This means that in order to get, say, 50% brightness, you move the handle to halfway between closed and 100% light, which is not necessarily the same as halfway of what the handle can move. On many lights in permanent installations, someone has marked along the edge of the douser with tape indicating, usually, 25%, 50%, 75% and 100% full brightness. Sometimes, only 50% is marked. These marks are usually made with little bumps of tape, or tape over a little piece of tie line or something, so you can feel where you are at without taking your eyes off the stage. Often, in a booth with a glass window, you can actually see how open your Douser is in the reflection of your light in the window. This is a useful benchmark. If your light is not marked and there is no useful reflection, it is a good idea, if you have time before the house opens, to pick up a wall somewhere on or near the stage, and mark brightness levels for yourself.

Strong Super Troupers, and other lights that have the douser closest to the lamp (and therefore heat) are prone to douser problems, as the plates distort a little from the heat. The heat from operation and then cooling off over and over can also tend to loosen the nuts holding the handle to the douser plates or the handle itself in place. They can usually be tightened without having to remove any plates or covers. On a Super Trouper, this is most easily accomplished with a ½" wrench. It is very common to see a ½" wrench sitting on a table or even tied to the light in a booth with Troupers. I keep one in my kit – many operators do. I like to stick it on the side of the light within reach with a magnet when I'm on a Trouper. It's a good idea, if you are fiddling with a douser nut in the middle of a show, to close the Chopper before operating on the douser. That way, you don't get accidental light leaks on stage as you work on it, and you can check the tension on the nut by moving the handle back and forth. Remember to close the Douser and open the Chop again before your next cue.

Some lights, particularly regular lighting instruments that have been shanghai'd into duty as a spotlight, Douse with a separate electronic control – either from the Light Board, or through a small dimmer or Variac transformer that the Operator controls. (See Non-Standard Spots – Chapter 4)

The Iris controls the size of the beam of your light. How big and small it can get. If you cannot get as large or as small as you need to at the extremes of the Iris, you may need to adjust the Trombone (Focus) on the light. The Iris has overlapping leaves that close like a camera shutter. On most lights, the Iris cannot close far enough to completely black out the light. On some models – most Juliats, for instance, it can. On many lights in permanent installations, someone has marked along the edge of the Iris with tape indicating, usually, Head Shot, Waist (or ½ body) Shot, Knee (or ¾ body) Shot, and Full Body. Sometimes, only Waist and Full are indicated. Like the Douser markings, these are often marked with bumps of tape so you can feel where you are at without having to look. Obviously, since performers come in different sizes, these are only ballpark marks. And, of course, if you are using a touring light, the throw distance may be different from their last venue, so any marks on the light are suspect. It is useful to mark these sizes, or at least an approximation of Waist and Full, on a light with no marks, if you can get to the light before the house opens. Many people mark the handle itself with a tape flag or some such so that it is easy to differentiate the Iris and the Douser by feel.

The direction that the Iris and Douser move to go from closed or small to open or big is different for different spotlight models. Even on lights that have control handles grouped together in the middle, it varies. On some models, Small on the Iris and Closed on the Douser are both accomplished with the handle away from the operator, moving to Big and Open respectively as they are pulled toward the operator. Sometimes the reverse. On other models, the Iris works one way while the Douser works the other. And which goes which way isn't consistent from manufacturer to manufacturer or even with different models from the same manufacturer. Also, where the Douser and the Iris and the Chop are in relation to each other changes from model to model. If you find yourself working on different lights in different venues a lot, it can take some getting used to. When you check out an unfamiliar light for the first time, it is vital to figure out which direction the controls work in, and how they are laid out. It is often useful to make little Gaff tape labels with "Open" or "Small" or whatever on them, and completely tape off the Chop. It may feel silly, but it's a lot better than grabbing the wrong handle or moving in the wrong direction in the middle of the show.

On lights where the Iris is closer to the lamp than the douser is, (many Lycian models, for instance) the Iris remain constantly exposed to the heat of the light and can often warp and distort over time. It is often good a good practice to open the Iris wide after firing up, between cues and overnight with these fixtures to extend the life of the Iris.

The Color Boomerang is where the gel colors for the spotlight go. Some spots have removable frames, others don't. If your spot has the type of frame that requires little brads to hold in color, it is a very good idea to flatten those brads as much as possible and use a small piece of gaff tape over the "ears" of the brad, so they won't bend up and start grabbing the frame next to them. If you get a choice, it is often wise to put the lighter colors closest to the lamp (and heat) and the darker, more saturated colors farther away. If you are using a frost, sometimes the placement in the boomerang can change the way the frost looks on the stage, and you may need to experiment with placement to get the look you want. The Handles on the Boomerang are numbered starting with the handle closest to the operator (closest to the lamp) at 1 and numbering away. Most spotlight boomerangs have 6 handles.

LD's and Spot callers use these numbers when they are telling you what color to put in. "Spot 1 in Frames 5 & 6, Spots 2 and 3 in Frame 3". Some operators mark the numbers on the handles, and if you find it helpful, you should absolutely do it. More common is someone putting a tab of tape on Frame 3 or 4, so you can feel it in the dark, and figure out other colors in relation to that by feel. A lot of people do both. If you haven't been given assigned colors, and/or you don't have anyone calling spots, it is often a good idea to write which color is in which frame on a little piece of Gaff tape or a post-it and stick it on the spot or nearby, so you know what's what.

Strong Gladiators, and possibly some other models of spots, have a 7th handle. On the Gladiator, this handle operates separately from the others, and is meant for a UV or Color correction filter, although it is often used for frost, or even just another color option. The frame installs backwards from the other frames, and therefore, you need its special frame if you are going to use the 7th handle. Many houses with Gladiators keep the special 7th Frames in a particular place and/or paint them a different color. It is possible, in a pinch, to tape a regular frame in upside down. If you try this, use a heat resistant tape rather than Gaff tape if you can. This 7th Frame does not release when you put in one of the 6 main colors, or with the color release lever for the main 6 colors. This is very helpful if you want to leave something – like color correction or frost – in for the whole show. The UV filter intended for this frame by Strong is made of glass and is heavier than a regular gel. Therefore, this handle has a stronger spring than the regular handles. So strong that you want to really watch your fingers when you release the color on that handle, as it comes banging down with force.

Juliat models also usually have a couple of frames for color correction or diffusion separate from the boomerang, generally controlled by small knobs near the center of the light.

Most Boomerangs are "self-cancelling". That is, when you put a color in, any colors that are already engaged are automatically released unless you hold them in place. This is a handy feature, since you can change colors by just putting the new ones in and allowing the old ones to fall. Depending on manufacturer, color handles either pull Up or Down to lock into place. To add a new color to one you already have engaged, you need to hold the "old" color that you are keeping in place as you add the new one. To drop one or more of a bunch of colors you already have in, you grab the ones you want to keep, and bump them a little farther in, allowing the other color(s) to drop out. All boomerangs have a release handle or button that will drop all colors. You only really need to use this to go to "Open White" or no color at all. (The 7th Frame on a Gladiator does not release with the handle that controls the other 6. This is very useful when you have a frost or color correction or some such that you want to keep in for all or most of the time. It has a separate release – and remember – watch your fingers!)

Some spotlight boomerangs, like at least one of the Juliat models, are not "Self-cancelling", and you have to add in or pull out individual colors manually. There is no release mechanism. This is fortunately pretty rare.

Some shows, particularly with small truss spots, will install a color scroller on the front of the spot. Sometimes the operator controls this, but more often, it will be controlled by the Light Board Operator.

Many spots are equipped with a slot cut into the bonnet of the unit near the focus gate. This "Drop Slot" can accommodate a color frame inserted from above. Lycian makes a two-color frame – one color at a time, but you can insert one end, or flip and insert the other for another color option, or no color, but

consistent weight balance. These frames for the slot are often called "dipstick frames" or just "dipsticks". This slot is most commonly used for Color Correction or Diffusion (Frost). It is sometimes used for a Gobo. Like the 7th Frame on a Gladiator, or the little knobs on a Juliat, it offers the option of another color that is not controlled by the release for the rest of the boomerang.

I've included a few simple drawings to try to illustrate some of the differences and similarities between some different popular brands of Spotlights.

Lycian 1293

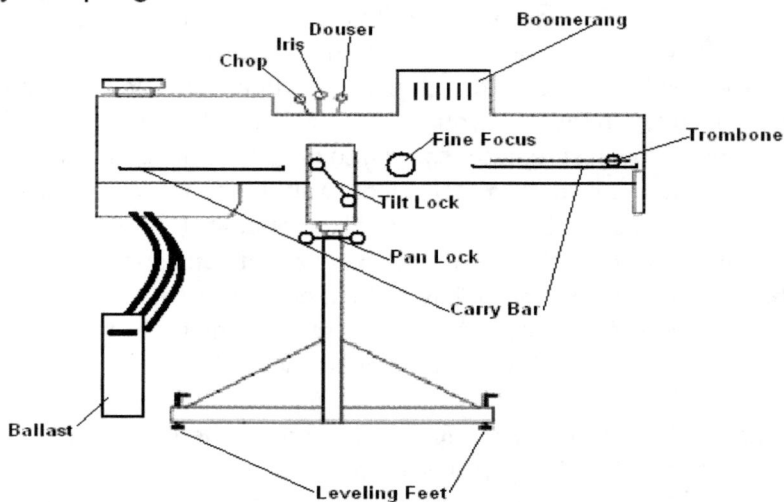

Lycian Spotlight

Strong Super Trouper

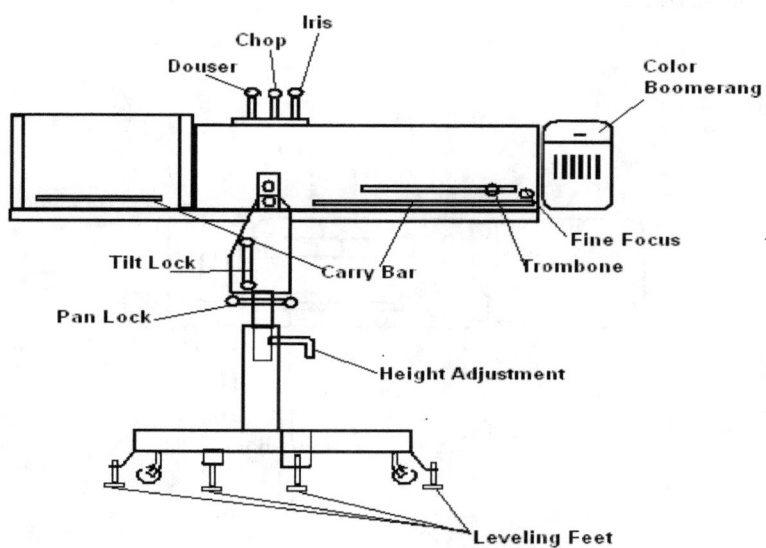

Juliat Cyrano

Juliat Cyrano

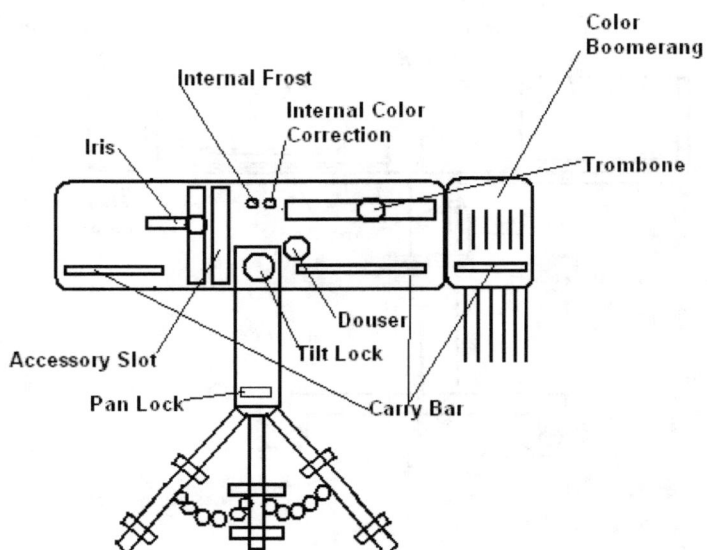

Color
Boomerang

Internal Frost

Internal Color
Correction

Iris

Trombone

Accessory Slot

Douser

Tilt Lock

Pan Lock

Carry Bar

12

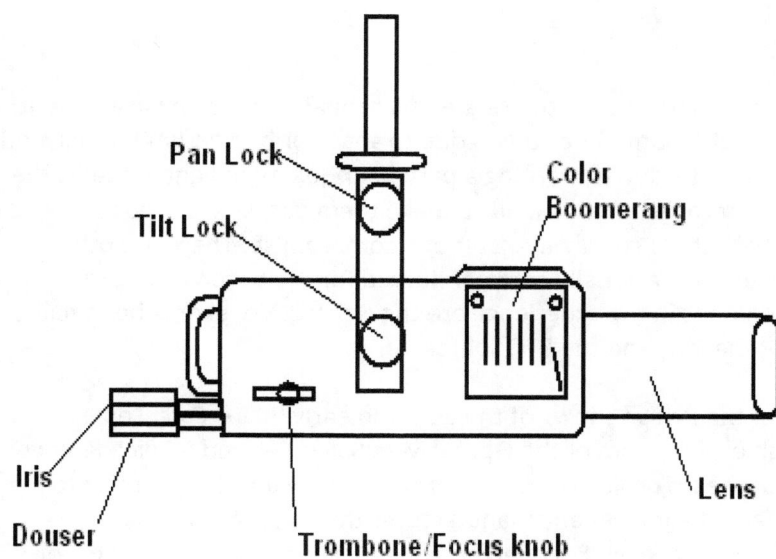

Pan Lock

Tilt Lock

Color Boomerang

Iris

Douser

Trombone/Focus knob

Lens

Chapter 3:
Non-Standard Spotlights

Often, designers choose to use a regular theatrical lighting instrument as a spotlight. Sometimes this is due to space or budget limitations, and sometimes, it's due to wanting a particular quality of light. Usually, the instruments are modified a bit to make them easier to use as a spotlight, but it's still always a bit of a compromise. There are other instruments occasionally commandeered for the purpose, but the most common ones in my experience are the Reich & Vogel or other small Beam Projector, and the ETC Source 4.

Many of the British shows of the 80's and early 90's – Cats, Les Misérables, Phantom of the Opera, Miss Saigon – used a Reich & Vogel 500-watt beam projector as a small spotlight. Many people refer to a small beam light from any manufacturer that is used this way generically as a Reich & Vogel (or, colloquially, a "Russian Vogel"), or just an RV.

RV's have a big soft light. It's an incandescent source, so it blends well with stage light. Because of that, and its soft edge, it can be used very effectively to basically highlight a performer within a scene, without giving the appearance of having an actual spotlight on them.

On the downside, because it is a big soft light, and there is no iris to control the size, spilling all over surrounding scenery can be a concern. Most shows attempt to control this to a degree by putting some kind of top hat or baffle or snoot on the front, but it only helps a little. It is possible to mount a color scroller on the light, but often, colors are just put in oversize frames and slid in and out like a standard color frame, safetied-off to the fixture or to a nearby railing. Sometimes, there's a little box to put them in so they aren't banging around.

There is no Douser on these units. The intensity of the light may be controlled by the lightboard, but often, they give the operator a little hand dimmer or Variac transformer. Some of those also have a toggle switch that you can use for an instant bump up or blackout if the show calls for something more specific than just spinning the dial up or down. (This is known as a "toggle bump"). It takes a bit of practice to get used to running the light with one hand and having the other on the intensity dial.

Another instrument commonly turned into a spotlight is an ETC Source 4. This practice is so common that vendors have come out with aftermarket attachments to help. You can buy swivels, irises, extra handles, and little color boomerangs to put in the gel frame slot on the front of the lamp. Using a source 4 this way has a lot of advantages. For one thing, it's probably something you can take out of existing inventory. And, you can fit it anywhere – on a catwalk, in a box boom slot, through a cove slot in the ceiling, etc. A variety of lenses are available, so you can pick your focal length. And, of course, it will blend well with the rest of your stage lighting.

On the downside, blending with the stage light means that it's hard to get it to punch out of the background when you want that. And, Source 4 lamps with a standard capacity, as far as I am aware at this writing, they can only take a maximum of a 750-watt lamp, so you are limited in how far away you can be and still get an effective throw. (It is possible to fit an HMI lamp or other source to a Source 4, but a modification like that would require a separate power supply, and an add-on douser, which would tend to nullify one of the main advantages of using an existing lamp.)

As with any other standard instrument, the intensity of a standard Source 4 can be controlled by the board or by the operator with a hand dimmer, and its color can be controlled by a color scroller operated from the board, or by the operator with gel frames or an aftermarket boomerang attachment.

When you douse a light by dimming the lamp up and down rather than using a physical douser, it takes a few seconds for the filament to completely fade after a fade out. If you move the light before that happens, you can leave a "comet tail" of light behind, which is generally undesirable. Spot callers will often warn you against this – "Fade out in place – no comets!"

Some shows, particularly in Rock & Roll, will use a moving light as a followspot. Typically, they disable the Pan and Tilt functions in the fixture and attach a small handle to the nose of the head for you to operate with. All other functions are controlled through the light board. Some shows will have a spot caller tell you when your light will be coming up, but often, they just give you a home person and have you follow that person continuously, whether your light is up or not, throughout the concert.

Some shows use automated lighting instead of, or in addition to, manually operated followspots by putting receivers on the performers that moving lights can track as the performers move around the stage. As of this writing, they are not widely used, as they don't offer the reliability, size control, and nuance that a human operator does, and they require a lot of programming and a dedicated set of moving lights. They tend to be seen in applications where subtlety is less important, like concerts and ice shows.

Some shows, particularly in Rock & Roll, use a remote "Ground Control" spot system. This allows an operator to control a moving light in the rig from a controller on the ground using a camera mounted on the fixture. The controller can be set anywhere – usually out of the way backstage or in a basement. The controller is laid out to resemble the controls on a conventional followspot and has a built-in sight. The operator has a monitor to watch the stage via the camera mounted on the associated fixture. The operator can control everything that they would on a standard followspot (Pan, Tilt, Color, Frost, Edge, Zoom) or a light board can control any or all of those functions. This system is a great alternative to truss spot positions. There is some associated lag time between movement of the controller and movement of the fixture. Most of the time, the operators can learn to account for this, but this lack of precision means that it will take some time and some upgrades before such systems see wide use in Theater, Opera, or Dance.

Chapter 4:
Spotlight Numbering

Usually, shows or venues assign a specific number to each spotlight, to make cue calling easier. On small informal shows, if they are called at all, the cue caller may just say "Roger, pick up the girl; Ted, pick up the boy" or whatever. But on bigger and/or busier shows, especially when the cue caller is a road person who doesn't necessarily know everyone's name, it is easier to use a number system.

There is no fixed system for the logic behind spot numbering. Often, the numbering starts with 1 farthest out in the house away from the stage, and number up as they move toward the stage. Sometimes, they number like conventional fixtures, from SL to SR. Sometimes they put Odd numbers on one side of the stage and Even numbers on the other. Within a booth, sometimes they start with 1 on one side of the booth or the other, but it is just as common to designate a Road Spotlight Operator as Spot 1 no matter where they are sitting, and number in whatever order is convenient to them from there.

Sometimes, a show will have some spotlights out in the Front of House, and other Truss Spots or Side Spots onstage. Sometimes they will use these terms to simplify cue calling or color changes, saying something like "Front Spots change to Frame 3, Onstage Spots change to Frame 6".

Sometimes, a show will put all the odd numbered spots on one side, and all the even numbered spots on the other side, or end of the arena. Often, they use this to simplify cue calling, saying something like "Even spots change to Frame 4, Odd spots change to Frames 2 and 3" or "Even spots on the Girl, Odd spots on the Boy". Sometimes a very complex show with many spots, like an Ice Show, will further designate everyone either an "X" or a "Y".

So, you may have 12 or 18 spotlights, and all the even numbered spots are on one side of the arena, and odd numbers are on the other, and

"X" spots are at the North end of the Arena, and "Y" spots are at the South end of the Arena. So, you might be Spot 3, **and** an Odd Spot, **and** an "X" Spot. It is often helpful to write this down on a piece of Gaff Tape or a Post it and stick it to your Spot, or your window, or the railing in front of you.

Chapter 5:
Stage Directions

On a stage, terms for which side is which and where things are located has a specific system. These directions are used by Stage Managers or other cue callers to tell you where your target is coming from, or where on the stage they are located. Sometimes they are used to tell you where they are in relation to some other performer or set piece.

On a traditional stage, the wall that separates the stage from the audience is called the Proscenium. Generally, you do not want your light to hit the Proscenium unless you are on a performer who is deliberately in front of it. The floor area in front of the Proscenium opening is called the Apron. Generally, you do not want your light to hit the front of the Apron edge, unless you have a performer sitting on the edge dangling his legs over or the like.

Stage Left is the left side of the stage from the performer's point of view – that is, standing on stage looking out at the audience. Stage Right is the right side from that point of view. Even if you are facing the other way, as spotlight operators usually are, Stage Left and Stage Right do not change. They remain Left and Right from the performer's perspective. This can take some getting used to, particularly if you don't work Front of House all the time. It is often helpful to put a little tab of tape on the window or railing in front of you, to remind you which side is which.

"House Right" and "House Left" refer to the sides of the stage from the audience point of view. These terms are very rarely used for Spotlights.

Upstage is toward the back wall of the theater, away from the audience. Downstage is toward the front of the stage, closest to the audience. These terms can designate and area of the stage, but also relative placement, like "Your guy is upstage of the sofa" or "Pick up the farthest downstage of the two ballerinas".

Upstage Left, then, is the Left side of the stage from the performer's point of view, away from the audience toward the back wall. Downstage Right is on the right side of the stage from the performer's perspective, down toward the front of the stage. Mid Stage Right or Left would be in the middle of the stage, neither Up or Down.

Center is the center of the stage in terms of right and left. "Center Line" is an imaginary line running from Upstage to Downstage, splitting the stage in half between Right and Left. Very often, a show will tape down a Center Line to help in placing the set and lighting focus. For some shows, particularly Dance, there may be a physical center line taped or painted on the floor or deck. If someone refers to "Center Center", they mean the very center of the stage, exactly halfway between the plaster line at the Proscenium and the back wall or back of the set, and along the Center line separating Stage Right and Stage Left.

Sometimes, particularly for Dance, a caller will refer to the "Quarter Line" – often "Quarter Line Left" or "Quarter Line Right". This is an imaginary line running from upstage to downstage splitting either the Stage Right or Stage Left side of the stage in half. Halfway between Center Line and the offstage wing. "Fade out when he reaches the quarter line on his way off Left".

Onstage and Offstage are usually used as relative terms. Onstage meaning closer to the Center line, Offstage meaning away from Center, toward the wings. As in "Spot 4, cheat your light Onstage a bit to get off that Proscenium wall" or "You are going to pick up Phil, in the blue, when he gets just Offstage of that doorway".

The areas all the way offstage on either side are called Wings. On many stages, there are masking curtains called legs that essentially divide the sides of the stage into separate entrances from the wings. Usually, you do not want to light the Legs themselves, fading out on an exiting performer before your light would hit the leg, or delaying pickup on an entering performer until they are clear. The farthest Downstage opening is called Wing 1, and they number up away from the audience, Wing 2, Wing 3, etc. Callers will often say "Your performer is coming on from Stage Left Wing 1" "You'll be picking your girl up in the Wing, Wing 2 Stage Right" or the like. Sometimes, this is shorthanded into "Left 2" or "Right 3". A cue sheet may reduce it even further, into a notation like

R1 or L2.

Wing 4 UPSTAGE Wing 4

Center Line

Wing 3 Wing 3

SR Center/Center SL

Wing 2 Wing 2

Wing 1 Quarter Line Right Quarter Line Left Wing 1

DOWNSTAGE

Proscenium Plaster Line Proscenium

APRON

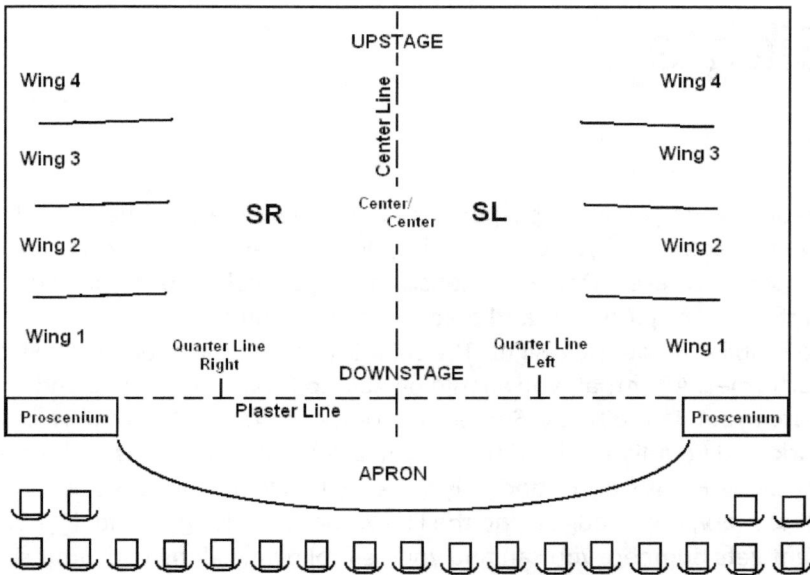

In a non-traditional performing space, like an Arena stage or Theater in the Round, traditional stage directions often have to be adapted or abandoned all together for a more practical system. Many round stages use a "clock" system, where they designate some given point as "12 O'clock" on an imaginary clock, and give other directions based on that. "12 O'clock" may be a specific aisle, or the light booth, or a set piece, or an exit sign. Any fixed marker, ideally, one that is clearly visible in the dark, can work.

Sometimes, particularly in an Arena or Theater in the Round, they will number aisles or doors and use those as reference points for pickups.

Chapter 6:
Sights

Ideally, when you pick up a performer, you are already in the correct size and color, and you pick up your performer exactly on target, properly centered. Doing this consistently, particularly on a moving performer, requires skill and practice. It is also much easier to accomplish if you use a sight. The sight is used for the initial pickup on a performer. After that, you should be able to pick your head up and watch your light directly. Sometimes, if a scene is very bright, or very dark, and your light is hard to see, you are stuck sort of chasing through the sight. But it's tiring, and only too easy to allow your light to splash on scenery, apron edges, and the like without realizing it. And, if your sight gets bumped, you can find yourself following along with your sight dead centered on the performer, while in reality, you light is tracking along to one side or the other. Try to get in the habit of using the sight only for the initial pickup.

There are old timers who scoff at using a sight at all, and for Rock and Roll type work, you can often get away with kind of Point and Shoot, ease in slowly and correct as you go. But for a lot of Theater, Opera, Dance, and even Concert work, that kind of sloppiness isn't acceptable. They require the kind of precision that you can really only achieve with a sight.

The classic way to hit a mark on stage is to use a whiteboard or blackboard hung in front of the spot. Most large spots have a strategic light leak – a pin hole in the center front of the lamp house that throws a tiny dot of light up above the spot. You pick up a particular spot on stage and mark the corresponding point that the pinhole throws up on your board – with a sharpie or a dry erase marker on a poster board or dry erase whiteboard, or with chalk on a blackboard. Then, whenever you line up your light leak with that mark, you should open in exactly the right place. Many operators mark out the edges of the stage and the center line when they first get up to the spot, which makes gauging other pickups much easier.

Even when I use a sight, I often find a target that will be possible to see during the show when the house is dark, like an Exit sign or the conductor's podium. When I have that place centered in my sight, I mark the whiteboard or blackboard. That way, if my sight gets bumped out of alignment, or I worry that it has, I can line up the mark on the whiteboard and check or reset my sight during the show without having to bring the light up at all.

Often, though, you are not conveniently located in a booth with the boards at hand or looking away from the stage to find your mark is not convenient. Or, your performer does not consistently hit a mark. In that case, it's easier to use a sight that doesn't require you to look away from the stage, that can be used in the open as well as in a booth. Operators have come up with many ingenious solutions over the years, and vendors have made commercial versions of many of them as well.

Many people build themselves some kind of standoff for their sights, so that it sits out a bit from the light, rather than forcing you to hug the light to make your pickup. Some commercial sights have standoff options. I hope it goes without saying that anything you attach to your light, especially if you are in the open rather than in a booth, should be securely tied off, or strapped, or at least taped down so that it can't fall. Frankly, the same goes for anything you carry up with you.

Coat Hanger Sight
One of the most basic sights is a Coat Hanger sight – a coat hanger disassembled into two pieces of wire. The end of one is generally bent into a loop, and the other left straight. You tape the straight piece upright to the very nose of your spot, and the loop farther back, closer to the operator, at the same height. You bring your light up on stage or a convenient wall and align the wires so that the straight piece in front is centered in the loop at the back when you look through them at your hot spot – the center of your light. During the show, you line up your sights on your performer, and when you open your Douser, they should be right in the center of your light. Variations on this, with pop can tabs, little flags of Gaff tape and the like are common.

Perfect Pick Up

A commercial version of the home-made coat hanger sight. It attaches to your lamp with a magnet. There is a standoff to hold it away from a light, and then a thin rod that folds out horizontal to the lamp with a small ring on the front end and a larger ring on the back end that you align with the hot spot of your lamp and lock in place. It travels folded up in a little tube.

Tube Sight

Another popular home-made sight, particularly helpful for smaller lamps and shorter throw distances, is a Tube Sight. You take a short piece (3" – 4") of tubing about ½" in diameter – either PVC, or conduit, or any other handy tube, and wrap it with either wire or plumber's strap so that you can stand it off from your light 3 or 4 inches. You attach it to the side of your light with either a magnet or tape, then bend it around until you are looking at the center hot spot of your light when you look through the tube.

Spot Dot

There is a The Spot Dot is basically a commercial version of the Tube Sight. The Spot Dot has the extra advantage of an illuminated red dot in the center, which gives you a much more precise center point than a plain tube. It has a built in stand off. The Spot Dot can also be used on a big light with a longer throw. It's small enough to stuff in a shirt pocket, which makes it particularly nice if you are climbing up to a truss or arena platform.

Daisy Sight

This is essentially a cheaper version of a Spot Dot. A tube sight with an illuminated red dot in the center. It is nicknamed the "Daisy sight" because it is actually made for use with Daisy BB Guns, although in reality, there are several manufacturers. Such sights can often be found in the Sporting Goods or Toy sections of big box stores or in outdoor stores. They are made to mount to a BB gun, so you have to McGyver yourself up a mount of some kind to put them on a spot.

Telrad

The Telrad is probably the most common sight used in Theater and Opera. The Telrad sight is a device originally manufactured for Star spotting and use with Telescopes. To this day, you can often find them through telescope dealers and catalogues at better prices than many theatrical suppliers. The Telrad has a fairly big window and a lit bulls-eye display which can dim up and down in brightness and is easy to see and use. Some people like to put a piece of light blue gel over the glass window to cut down glare and make the target easier to see in a bright scene. It has 3 alignment screws on the back to help align the bulls-eye with the center Hot Spot of your light. The center of the bulls-eye is open, so you aren't obliterating your target. It has a separate base, which can be attached to a spot with either tape, or magnets, or even Velcro. Stand-off bases are also commercially available. The bases come with a peel and stick tape on them, but unless you are going to be leaving it on one spot permanently, it doesn't make much sense to use that. Also, the adhesive doesn't stay particularly well – a couple of large pieces of Gaff tape over the base or magnets screwed to the base are a better bet.

Rifle Scope
Many people like to use a rifle scope for a sight – particularly for precise pickups in a low light situation. Rifle scopes usually magnify the image, which makes it easier to see, and also gather light, which is very helpful on a dim stage. I prefer a 4 X 32 sight. It gives me enough magnification to be useful, but not so much that it makes adjustment difficult.
The down side of magnification is that it takes a moment for your eyes to adjust from the magnified image in the scope to the regular view, and you can lose your target while your eyes adjust, particularly if your target is on the move. You can buy scopes with more or less magnification (or none), or larger or smaller lenses. (The "4" tells you how much magnification it has. The "32" refers to the size of the scope's front lens. Some people prefer a "[whatever] x40 or even x50" lens. The larger the number, the bigger the lens, and therefore, the easier to look through and the more light gathering potential it has.) I don't like the zoom or varifocal scopes for spotlight work. The extra lenses mean you lose brightness, and the extra hassle of focus isn't usually worth the result. They tend to be heavier and more expensive than the fixed lens variety, too.

Some people recommend looking for a waterproof model. Otherwise, you may end up with issues of clouding on the lenses, particularly in a humid environment. Some people like to get a scope made to have "Extended Eye Relief". Such scopes are made to be looked through from a little farther back, so you don't need to press your eye right up to the sight. Pistol sights are often made with a long eye relief.

All such bells and whistles mean added expense, however. You need to balance what features you want to have in a rifle scope with what you are willing to spend, and what size you are willing to carry. The weight can become a significant factor too, as you figure out how to mount it on to a spotlight without allowing it to slip. Adding features can ratchet up the price of a scope significantly, and for most of what we do, a lot of the extras tend to be a bit of overkill.

You can make a mounting base for it out of either the clips meant to hold it on a rifle, or clips for a C-cell flashlight. Some people use small hose clamps, or even zip ties to hold it to some kind of base or standoff.

Chapter 7:
Balance

Balancing the light – that is, adjusting the level and weight so that it will stay where you put it when its locking controls are completely released, is probably the single most important thing you can do to prepare the spotlight when you get there. A badly balanced light will wear you out in short order, constantly fighting it as the nose attempts to fly to the ceiling or drop to the floor, or just drifts off to one side. If you literally cannot take your hands off the light the whole night, it can be an exhausting (and hot!) experience. Taking time to balance your light can make all the difference in doing a good job.

After you have set the Trombone, put colors in the Boomerang and Slot, and added any sights, handles, com belt pack, or other accessories to a light, you should check that the spot is sitting stable and level. Spot booth floors are notoriously uneven. Sometimes sliding your spot just a little bit one way or another can help enormously. You definitely don't want it rocking back and forth, and an unlevel spot can make the head pull one way or the other. To check, release the locking handle for the Pan (side to side). If the light veers off to one side or another, try adjusting the leveling feet on the stand of the light. (This often requires a wrench, or even pliers or Channel-Locks). If they are not present or it's not practical, try shimming a low side up. Ideally, the light should stay put when released.

Once you are happy there, release the locking handle for the Tilt. Again, you want it to stay in place when you release it. You want it to stay pointed toward the stage, which is usually somewhat below you, so it is often good to have the light a little front heavy. Some fixtures, like the big Lycian models, have a sliding weight built in to the front of the light that you can slide forward or back and lock in place. Most of the time, you end up making your own adjustments with whatever is handy, by hanging weight on either the front or back of the light with tie line. It is very common to use a bundle of spare gel frames, or shackles or C-clamps or whatever iron may be lying about. I keep a short length of chain in my bag. It works as a weight, and piles into the bag without taking up much room. A lot of people use a bottle of water as a weight. You can adjust the weight by pouring (or drinking) off some water until you get the weight you like. Some operators carry 3 or more pairs of vice grips in different sizes. They can be a quick way to add weight on to the lamp for Balance and won't swing around like an object tied on to the light can. Between having different sizes and being able to choose how far forward or back on the light (Usually on the carry bar) you clamp them, you can have good control over your weight balance.

If a light is very badly out of balance, and needs a large amount of weight to keep from flying up or down, you should mention it to the folks in charge of maintaining the spots for the house, because on many models, it is possible to adjust the way a lamp sits in the yoke to help fix this problem. Day to day, you should only need enough weight to compensate for whatever color or accessories you have put in. Your ultimate goal is to be able to take your hands off of the light completely, and have it stay in place.

In the old days, operators would lock off their light to hold it in place for a long scene or song, often with unhappy results as an actor unexpectedly took off, or the operator just forgot to unlock before the end of the song. There are operators who would lock their light off for a long scene and then wander off to the bathroom or whatever. This is extremely bad unprofessional behavior, and you should never do it. Never leave your light unattended when it is open on the stage.

Chapter 8:
Firing the Lamp

Once you have put color in the light, added your sight, handles, or other accessories, and Balanced the light, you are ready to fire up the lamp. Different models of lights have different ways of firing up, and different venues set things up their own way as well. First, make sure the Douser is closed – you don't want to fire up and have sudden unexpected light blasting the stage. Make sure your light is plugged in – this sounds simplistic, but in some Houses, where breakers are not easily accessible, they kill Ballast power at night by simply unplugging it. If the breakers for the Spotlight power are in the Spotlight booth or easily accessible, and they have been turned off, turn them on. Most spotlights have some kind of Ballast for transforming and/or conditioning power, and it often has a separate on/off switch or breaker. Sometimes, the ballast is built into the light, and the switch will be located there. Not all Ballasts have a switch – some will turn on when you plug them in or give them power from a breaker, although they may have a breaker of their own. Most lights will have a separate switch or buttons to actually fire the light. So, the spotlight plugs to ballast (if there is one) which plugs into the wall. Power for the wall outlet may be controlled by a breaker or switch in the booth, the ballast may have a power switch or a breaker, the spotlight may have a power switch, and either the ballast or the spot may have the buttons or switches to turn the lamp itself on and off.

Some small spotlights do not have a separate ballast, and may use a simple rocker switch to turn the lamp On and Off again. Most larger lamps will separate the Power On/Off function that controls the internal ballast and fans from the Lamp On and Lamp Off Buttons that control the lamp itself.

Many Strong Lamps (Super Trouper, Trouper II, Gladiator) have a "Mode" switch on the back of the lamp, which allows you to set a spotlight to "Auto" mode – where the light can be triggered remotely, from a light board or whatever, and "Man" mode – manual mode, where the light is triggered directly by the operator. Most of the time, the "Man" mode is what you want. Check that this switch is in the correct position before firing.

Once you have power, and the ballast is on so that you have fans blowing and power prepped, hold the lamp head level, and push your "On" button to fire the lamp. This button is often Red. It may be marked "On" or "Strike" or "Lamp" or something similar. It may be located either on the ballast, or on the lamp head. Most arc lamps fire up with an audible "zap" or "click". Sometimes, on an older lamp, you will hear two or three attempts before the lamp actually fires.

If your lamp won't fire after you hear two or three attempts, turn it off by pushing the other button, which is often Yellow and may be marked "Off" or "Standby". Tip the nose of the lamp up to the ceiling and back down to the floor a time or two. The thinking is that this will help mix the gasses in the lamp. Some people scoff at this explanation, but for whatever reason, it seems to help. Return the lamp to horizontal and try firing again.

Once you have fired up a lamp, it should run for a minimum of 15 or 20 minutes before being powered down again. There will be some kind of switch to kill the lamp. Sometimes, just the "off" position of an "On/Off" rocker switch that fired the lamp. More usually, particularly with a big light, a separate switch or button as described above ("Off" or "Standby") which kills the lamp but leaves the fans running. Once powered down, it should really get a minimum of an hour or so of rest before it gets struck again, for maximum lamp life. (And since Xenon Spotlight lamps can cost anywhere from about $500 to $1,000 or more apiece, depending on wattage and manufacturer, preserving lamp life is important.) Spotlight lamps are intended to be run continuously throughout a show or event. Don't power down the spot at intermission, or for any breaks of less than an hour.

When you power down a big Xenon light, you should leave fans running for a minimum of 10 – 15 minutes. A forced air-cooling cycle is actually required by all bulb manufacturers that I am aware of. This is important, because even after you shut off a lamp, particularly if it is deprived of fan cooling, it will actually build heat sitting inside the lamp house. You need to give it enough time with the fans helping to draw off heat that it is on the way to cooling down before you kill Ballast power (and therefore, fans). Generally, you wait until there is no visible glow from the lamp, and the lamp house is not very hot to the touch before powering down the Ballast.

Some houses have installed a timer switch, which will allow cool down time without the operators having to wait around. Other houses control the Ballast power from a remote location, like the Light Booth or backstage, so that operators can walk away after the show. Whatever the case, you should check with your supervisor to see what the procedure is in that venue for lamp cool down and powering off.

Chapter 9:
Lamp Safety and Troubleshooting

Xenon lamps, the type used in many large followspots, have some safety considerations for the operator. You should never view an operating lamp directly, and indeed, it is nearly impossible to do so. Lamp houses are heavily secured, usually with some kind of security screws, for good reason. Most also have some kind of safety switch that will extinguish a lamp if the cover is loosened. There is no reason for you, as an operator, to need to open a lamp house, whether the lamp is lit or not. Some fixtures have a little "window" on the side of the lamp house that allows you to see if your lamp is operating or not.

Xenon lamps are highly pressurized, and if they do blow, they explode OUTWARDS, sending tiny shards of glass everywhere. Anyone who has ever had the misfortune to have a bulb explode in a lamp they are running will tell you that the noise is tremendous – it sounds like a bomb going off behind your head, which is pretty much the case. Hot lamps are MUCH less stable and more dangerous than room temperature lamps, but even a room temperature lamp is under a dangerous amount of pressure and should not be handled without protective clothing including a face mask, gloves, and some kind of protective jacket. Most manufacturers recommend a heavy leather jacket like welders wear. As an operator, you should never really need to deal with lamp installation, and if someone qualified is installing a lamp or has the lamp house open for any reason, stay well clear.

Lamps should be adequately ventilated. This is particularly vital for Carbon Arc Spotlights, which usually have the exhaust stack from their lamp house directly connected to a forced air exhaust system, but even Xenon lamps need some ventilation. Some venues that have converted from Carbon Arc spots to Xenon lamps hook the new lamps up to the old ventilation system, and it's not a bad idea – it can help to draw off heat from the lamp, certainly.

Even if a lamp is not directly hooked to an exhaust system, having exhaust fans in a booth to draw off heat and help encourage proper air flow through the fixture is a good idea. When Xenon lamps were first introduced, there was some concern because the radiation from some xenon bulbs can convert the oxygen in the surrounding air to ozone. In large quantities, ozone can endanger health, but it spontaneously changes back into oxygen in a very short time, especially if it mixes with a large volume of air (as in an auditorium, arena, or outdoors). Most currently manufactured xenon bulbs are classified as *ozone free* and do not release ozone. Still, proper ventilation, particularly in a closed booth type environment, is a good idea.

For most operators, any operational trouble with your lamp, like flickering, low output, Hot Spot of the light centered badly, etc. is something that you just endure during a show, and then report to your superiors and let them deal with. If your lamp is not working at all, you would obviously want to tell whoever is in charge, but there are a few things that you can check while you're there:

PROBLEM	CHECK
No power – no lights, no fans	Make sure Ballast is plugged in to the wall

Make sure Ballast is plugged into lamp head

Make sure Breaker or "On" switch for the Ballast is On

Make sure any Breakers for the plugs are On, and not tripped

Check that you have power at the plug either by using a meter, or by plugging another spot or ballast into the plug if available |
| Power at Ballast, lamp will not strike | On a Strong lamp (SuperTrouper, Gladiator, etc.) check that the "Auto/Man" switch next to the lamp On/Off switch in the back of the lamp is set to "Man"

Turn off, tip lamp up and down a few times, bring back to horizontal, try again

Many lamps have an air pressure or cover switch which will prevent strike if air is restricted or the housing around the lamp comes loose. Check cover and fans. |
| Lamp extinguishes after it has been running, no power | Check that plug has not been kicked out

Check connections between wall, ballast, and lamp

Check breaker for the wall

Check breaker and/or power switch on ballast

Check breaker and/or power switch on the unit |

Lamp extinguishes after it has been running, power, lights, and fans still operating	Check for loose power connections
	Many lamps have an air pressure or airflow switch which will turn the lamp off if air is restricted or the housing around the lamp comes loose.
	Make sure nothing is blocking any fans
	Make sure fans can turn freely – it is not uncommon for the little wire grate over a fan to get bent in to where it is touching the fan and preventing it from turning properly – particularly underneath the lamp, where an operator's knee could be the culprit.
	Make sure the lid to the lamp housing is securely in place
	Make sure lamp is venting properly – check that any exhaust fans attached to the lamp or in the booth are on.
	Let lamp cool a bit before attempting restrike
	If the Lamp "On" switch is still in place or illuminated, turn it off before trying to strike again.

Chapter 10:
Intercom

In many venues, spotlight operators are responsible for plugging their headsets into the Intercom (usually just called "com") system when they go up to a light. Some places have dedicated headsets and belt packs that they leave in a spot booth or at spot positions, but many don't. Many road shows will have the sound department set up the com for the spots, but again, many don't. Sometimes you're just handed a milk crate full of stuff and sent on your way.

Generally, either a line will be run to your position, or a line run to a little box with connectors in the spot booth or near your positions, or there will be jacks in the wall to plug into. Usually, you have a cable to run from the wall or line to a connector on a belt pack, and your headset plugs in to another connector on the belt pack. These jacks are usually different from each other – either different types of connectors or at least different numbers of pins, making it impossible to plug your headset into your feed jack or vice versa. Sometimes, several operators will be "Daisy Chained" from a single feed or jack, so the feed from the wall goes into the first belt pack, and you will have cables to go out of the first belt pack and into the second, out of the second and into the third, and so on.

So, a belt pack may have several connection options on the bottom. Typically, a male recessed jack to take the connector for the cable running from the wall or the previous person's belt pack to your belt pack, and a female of the same type to attach a daisy chain cable out of your pack to feed the next guy if you are going to be set up that way. Also, some kind of male recessed jack for your headset cable to plug into. Often, your headset cable "locks" in, and you must press a button next to the connector or on the side of the belt pack to release your headset cable. If you have a multi-channel belt pack, there will be more connections available.

Many operators like to carry a personal headset, which is often lighter weight and in better condition than the one you may be issued by the venue. Different intercom systems have different types of jacks and pin configurations for the headset, so you need to make sure that yours has either the right kind of connector for the venues you mostly work in, or an adaptable connector that can work on different systems. Also, different systems require different types of microphones. Some belt packs require a condenser microphone, some an electronic one. Some belt packs are switchable. If your headset or your microphone is not working with the system, consult whoever is in charge of Intercom. Many venue TDs, sound guys and road people are suspicious of personal headsets, worried that yours will cause some kind of problem or interference with their system.

As you are running cables for your Com, take care not to let them run alongside power cables for your lamp, or around the Ballasts or other electrical supply. If Headset cables have to cross over power cables, it is better for them to cross each other at a perpendicular angle than run alongside each other. Headset cables being too close to power cables is a common reason for Hum in the headset, which can be really annoying and make hearing what you need to hear difficult.

The belt packs are made to be worn on your belt, but it is often easier to clip them to your spot (some models have a place for this) or clip them to a loop of tie line tied off to your yoke or carry bar, or tied to a railing near you. If you have a music stand handy, you can clip it to that. You want to be able to see the mic button, so you can see if it is on or off and reach it easily.

Usually, they have two buttons on the top – one is your "talk" button, that you push to activate your mic and talk. On many models, one push and hold lets you talk, a quick double push locks the mic on. You may have one button marked "PTT", which stands for "Push to Talk", and is usually a momentary switch, that only works when you are actively pushing it. On these types of headsets you usually have another button marked "Hold" or "Lock" or something, which locks your mic on. As an operator, you would hardly ever want to lock your mic on, and you should check from time to time to make sure you haven't done so inadvertently. There is usually a light telling you if the mic is on or not. DEFINITELY check to make sure your mic is off before moving the boom for your microphone, even a little. Racking your mic boom from in front of your mouth to over your head or vice versa with the mic on makes an insanely loud noise in everybody else's headset and will upset everyone. Don't do it.

The other button typically found on the belt pack is the "call" button. When the call button is pushed on any one pack, it lights up the call light on all the packs on that system. Sometimes, a spot caller or SM will hit the call light to get someone's attention and ask them to pick up if they have taken off a headset. Sometimes, a call light is used to cue a particular action. Most of the time, as a spot operator, you just want to avoid accidentally hitting the call button when you meant to hit the mic button.

There is usually a little wheel to control volume on the belt pack. This wheel controls the volume of what you HEAR. It has no effect on the volume of your microphone. It sometimes seems like it does, because by increasing the volume of what you are hearing, you hear yourself louder too. But others do not. If there are complaints that you are hard to hear, the easiest and most common fix is to move the microphone (WITH THE MIC OFF!!!) closer to the front of your mouth. Speaking up helps, of course. In a very loud environment, like a rock concert, cupping your hand behind the mic when you speak helps a lot. If you are getting complaints that you are too loud, you can try the reverse – moving your mic (OFF!!!) a little away from your mouth down on your chin. Some belt packs have a Hi-Lo switch for microphone volume on the bottom, and if you are consistently too loud or too soft for everyone else, you can try switching this to the other setting.

Some belt packs have the capacity to feed show program to you through the headset. Packs with this capability usually have a little volume knob or wheel on the bottom of the belt pack to adjust how loud that show feed is in your headset.

Some spot booths have speakers for show sound set up, and you may need to turn these on or adjust their volume when you get up to the booth.

Chapter 11:
Iris Sizes

Below are some terms used to specify the size of the beam of light (controlled by the followspot's iris):

Pin Spot – as tiny as your Iris can go without closing off the light completely.

Head Shot – Sized to pick up just a performer's head. Very often, this is as small as the Iris will go. Usually, a head shot includes any hat or headdress that a performer may be wearing.

Head and Shoulders – Slightly larger than a Head Shot, as the name implies, including the whole head and the shoulders of a performer. Sometimes, depending on throw, focus, and etc., this may be as small as your Iris will go.

Waist Shot – This is lighting the top half of a performer – from the Waist up. Generally, it means that the bottom of your beam lands at the belt line, and your hot spot is up on the performer's face. Some callers and designers prefer that you cheat the hotspot down a bit to limit the amount of excess light going over a performer's head and lighting up scenery.

Half Body – Generally, the same as a Waist shot. Callers tend to use one term or the other. Sometimes, a half body means including a specific piece of costume, like a suit coat, or even including the performer's hands at his side, although you would usually want a larger size for that.

Knee Shot – As the name implies, lighting a performer from the Knees up. This size is often used when they want to include an actor's hands, or give him a little more room to maneuver, but don't want the spill of extra light that a Full Body size would produce. For a shot this big, you really have to cheat the hot spot of your light down a little bit from a performer's face. You want to keep his face in light, but don't want to blow a ton of light over his head and all over the scenery.

3/4 Body – Generally, the same as a Knee shot. Callers tend to use one term or the other. Sometimes, 3/4 means a little less than a Knee shot – big enough to include an actor's hands at his sides, or the bottom of a suit coat or other costume piece, but not fully open to the Knees.

Full Body – As the name implies, the Full Body of the actor, including his feet. Generally, although you have to cheat your hot spot down from the actor's face a bit, you still want to stay a little high. Even at full body, a performer's face is usually more important than their feet. You have to balance getting enough light on their face, while still including their full body, against the amount of extra light that you blow over their head and around them to accomplish it.

Generous Full Body/Big Full Body – Terms used by some callers to tell you to stay big, leaving the performer a little room to maneuver. This is often a good idea for Stand-up Comedians, who have a tendency to pace, or anyone using a large prop, or anyone who tends to make sudden moves. It is usually more attractive to let someone fidget about within your light rather than trying to stay tight and follow all their individual little moves.

Two-shot – A term borrowed from Film and Television. This means to include two performers in one single spotlight. This is occasionally adapted to "Three-shot", and so on.

Chapter 12:
Intensities and Fade Counts

Whoever is calling cues to spots will usually give you an intensity – how bright the spot should be. Sometimes, this is easy – you may be at 100% Full Intensity for every pick up in a presentational show like a Rock and Roll concert. Sometimes, it's absurdly nit-picky, with designers who are more used to the precision of digital lighting consoles than the handles on a typical spotlight, and they are asking for intensities like 38%, or 79%. There is no real way to achieve anything this precise unless you have a dimmer or Variac of some kind to control your light with.

Usually, experienced spot callers try to stick to intensities that you can reasonably eyeball on the fly, but still give them a good range of choices. Most often, they express this in terms of percentages, like 25%, 50%, 75%, 100%. Sometimes, they will throw in other intensities, like 35% or 85%, to try to squeak in a look that doesn't quite match one of the rounder numbers. Sometimes, for a very low light pick up, they may ask for a "Glow" or 10% or 15% in addition to the other choices. Some callers express intensities as 1/4 intensity, 1/2 Intensity, 3/4 Intensity, or Full Intensity rather than as percentages. Some will go with 1/3 or 2/3 in addition or instead.

To an extent, the levels are based on how open and closed your douser is, which you can figure from calculating divisions of the travel of your handle between closed and Full Intensity. It is important to remember that the handle may well have a bit of travel left even after you have reached Full, and this part doesn't count. 50% is halfway between closed and Full intensity, not half of actual handle travel. Often you can see the progress of your douser in the reflection of your light in a spot booth window.

The position of your douser isn't everything, however. The size of your iris can affect the brightness of your light quite a bit. This effect is more pronounced with smaller lights, and when you are closer to the target.

Often, you can achieve more brightness just by opening up your size a bit. Also, you may find that as you tighten your iris, you need to open your douser to maintain the intensity that you have had. And, of course, the reverse.

If you are running a truss spot on stage, or any spot at one end of a long arena, your light will get smaller and brighter as you come closer to yourself and get bigger and dimmer as you move farther away. You often need to open and dim as they get close, and tighten and brighten as they move away, to maintain a consistent look across the stage.

In a less concrete zone, perception has a lot to do with it, and contrast has a lot to do with it. Your light can seem a lot brighter in a dim scene than it does in a bright one, and one caller's 35% may be someone else's 50%.

Fade Counts

Timing for spotlight pick-ups and fade outs is generally expressed as "counts", which roughly equate to seconds. An instant pick up, banging on like someone has hit a light switch, is called a "Bump" or "Bump Up". Sometimes called a "0 count". An instant fade out, the same thing in reverse, is called either a "Bump Out" or a "Blackout". Sometimes, this is what you want, for a specific effect, or in a presentational rock show or pageant.

Usually, unless you are given specific instructions otherwise, you want to Fade-In and Fade-Out on your people in a smoother manner, more like a 2 or 3 count Fade. There are often cues where they will ask for a specific count – like a 5 or 10 count fade up or out. Sometimes, when there are several spots doing a simultaneous fade, particularly a long one, the caller will count it out for you, to ensure that everyone works together.

For the record, if someone asks you to Fade-Out in 5 counts, they want you to start when they say "Go" and take 5 seconds to reach complete out. They do not intend for you to wait 5 seconds after they say "Go" and then bump out.

Chapter 13:
Fall Arrest

Let me first say that I am not a rigging expert or a Fall Arrest expert. Don't take my word as law for any of this - there are a variety of rigging companies, books and resources on the web and elsewhere that have tons of useful information on this stuff. OSHA offers their OSHA 10 and OSHA 30 courses that include good information in this area. My goal in this section is to try to acquaint you with the basics of what to look for in a Fall Arrest system, and perhaps get you interested enough to check out your questions with a real expert. Please don't declare something good or not, or especially legal or OSHA compliant or whatever or not, based on my descriptions. I'm trying to give you benchmarks to look for to keep yourself safe, not absolute rules and regulations.

Many times, spotlight operators are asked to climb up to a truss or catwalk that requires you to wear fall protection. When are you required to wear it? Well, the short form, as I understand it, is: any time you are going to be over six feet high without adequate railings.

What constitutes "wearing fall protection"? You need to be wearing a harness – and not just any harness, but an OSHA compliant Full Body Fall Arrest Harness with a sliding D-ring in the upper back. To ensure that you have a Legal Fall Arrest Harness, check the label. It should say that it meets or exceeds ANSI code requirements, and it will cite a specific code number. **It has to be full body, and it has to have the ring in the upper back.** Various models also have rings on the chest, or at the belt, or on the hips, but those are for positioning, not Fall Arrest.

A rock-climbing sit harness is not legal. People often use these, but they aren't meant for Fall Arrest, and if you are in an accident, OSHA will cut you no break for wearing an inappropriate harness. If a road show hands you one of these to use for Fall Arrest, just say no.

Unless you are hooking straight into a Retractable Life Line, you should also have a lanyard, attached to your Dorsal Fall Arrest Ring in the upper back. Again, there are legal and not legal Lanyards. A legal one, for Fall Arrest purposes, is no more than 6 feet long, and will often have shock absorber built in. (A Lanyard with a built in Shock Absorber is often called a Manyard). There are a couple of different styles of shock absorber available. There are many nicknames for these – Zorber, Zipper, and Screamer (it makes a noise when deployed) are some I've heard.

Should you buy your own harness and lanyard? Well, if you do a lot of overhead work, it's not a bad idea. At least then, you'll have one sized to fit you, whose straps and buckles you understand, and you know its history. Realize that if you are providing your own harness and/or lanyard, you are assuming responsibility for maintenance and inspection, and taking the on the liability for any failure on the part of your gear in the event of a fall. For these reasons, some venues and some shows want you to wear their harnesses, because they know those are legal, they know their history, it's their insurance, and it keeps the liability on the show or venue. This makes sense to me, and if they look to be in good shape, I'll wear them. If they are providing the harness, there should be someone there to show you how to put it on and make sure that it is buckled properly.

Next, you have to hook off **to** something. Every part of the system, and especially, whatever you are tying off to, must be able to support 5000 pounds. (This accounts for the weight of you and your gear, but also the "jerk weight" of your weight hitting the end of a 6' lanyard, which can be substantial. 5000 pounds may seem like overkill, but then, there are some things worth over-engineering a bit.) A lighting truss very often has a Horizontal Life Line running along the top to clip into. Some installations will have vertical lifelines hanging overhead instead. The important thing is that you are hooked off to something at all times.

Before you clip into your ultimate hook off point, however, you have to get there. If you are climbing a ladder, you need to clip to something on the way up. One common solution is a vertical rope or cable grab to hook into that rides up a line next to the ladder when you are ascending, but will "grab" and catch you if you fall. I have usually seen these on fixed ladders in permanent installations. The other usual choice is a Retractable Lifeline. Although these come in a variety of sizes and styles, one very common one is the "Teardrop" style with retractable wire rope, often called a "Yo-yo".

An important note, which is rarely mentioned in Fall Arrest literature, is that **Retractable Lifelines are designed to be clipped directly into your Dorsal (Upper Back) D-Ring. NOT connected to your lanyard, especially if your lanyard has a shock absorber.** While you might think that attaching the Retractable Lifeline to your shock absorbing lanyard is somehow "super safe", there are a couple of reasons why this is not so. First, most Retractable Lifelines will give you a little slack before they engage – up to a foot or so. Getting jerked up short like that will be uncomfortable, but better than falling. However, if you add 6' of lanyard to that, then the shock of a fall goes from uncomfortable to quite painful. Worse, if 6' of lanyard, plus a foot or so of retractable lifeline, could let you hit the floor. But, you say, the shock absorber is there to prevent me from getting a sudden hard shock. While this is true, the shock absorber relies on having a fixed point to pull against in order to do its job, and a Retractable Lifeline relies on being able to catch you short, before you take a big fall. A series of tensioning jerks and releases from a shock absorber can allow the retractable lifeline to release and catch again, over and over. Also, in the act of deploying, the shock absorber adds length to your lanyard. This stopping and starting with an increasingly longer lanyard can be very bad and painful, and depending on how close you are to the floor, worse.

Another good reason to attach a Retractable Lifeline directly to your D-ring is that it leaves your lanyard free for you to hook off to a Horizontal Lifeline or other attachment point on the truss or catwalk **before you unhook the Retractable Lifeline**. You want to stay clipped off at all times, and the point where you transfer from ladder to truss or whatever is a particularly precarious position. Not a good time to unclip from protection. If you are going to be transferring from one attachment point where you need a lanyard to another, you need a double lanyard. You can use a manufactured "Double Lanyard," or use a harness with two D-rings with a lanyard on each. It is not sensible to unclip from one area of protection before you have attached yourself to the next one.

What if they don't have harnesses available? What if no one else is wearing one? What if everybody is wearing sit harnesses? What if, what if, what if . . . If the safety gear isn't available, don't do the climb.

Chapter 14:
Spot Bag

Every good spotlight operator eventually gathers a little kit of stuff they like to have with them when they are on a spotlight call. Typically, they contain your sights, handles, gloves, and other accessories and tools. It's a good idea to keep the things you want in your Spot Bag separate from whatever other tools you carry or usually bring to a call, so you can just grab it and go when you are sent up to a spotlight. What rides in your spot kit tends to be pretty individual. Everyone has their own preferences, different venues and different types of calls call for different things, and you weigh what you need to have against what you are willing to carry around.

Representative List:

Sight(s) – I often have a couple of different sights in my bag, as some work better than others for any given situation. If you know what you are getting into before you arrive, or you are working at a house where they have sights permanently installed on the lights, you may carry one or none.

Stand off – for the sight or sights you are carrying. I like to have something to stand the base of the sight off of the light a bit, so I don't have to hug the light so closely for pickups.

Batteries – Many sights use batteries for power, and you should always have backups with you for any sights that you carry. It doesn't hurt to have spare batteries for your flashlight, either.

Gloves/Arm protection – Spotlights get hot as you run them – some models hotter than others. Many operators like to wear a glove on their left hand to help protect fingers from the heat. Some people don't like wearing a glove, since it makes it harder to feel where you are for sizes and intensities. Particularly on a big light, many operators like to wear some kind of protection for their left forearm in addition to or instead of a glove. One way to protect yourself is to put something over the edge of the light next to the controls. A mouse pad taped in place is popular, as is carpet, or even a doubled over towel. Many operators have some kind of sleeve for that arm – for instance, a sleeve cut off an old sweatshirt, a long oven mitt with the hand part cut off, a leather welding glove with the hand cut off, or an archery gauntlet. It is possible to get a glove and forearm gauntlet in one piece. Some theatrical suppliers sell these, but it is more common to find them in an Archery supply place, or a place that sells gardening products. (Look for a "Rose glove").

Handles/Vice Grips – Some operators like to have a separate handle, usually attached to the long carry bar in the front of the light, to give them something easier and more ergonomic to grab than the carry bar itself. It is much better to use an external handle than to use the Trombone handle to move the light. Pulling on the Trombone can weaken the brake on it, and possibly cause it to pull loose and change your size and disrupt your focus during a cue. Extending a handle out from the carry bar can help you keep your back in better alignment as you run the light and watch the stage. Some small lights benefit from an extra handle on the back or on the bottom. Some theatrical suppliers carry handles, but more commonly, Operators make them out of a pair of vice grips or some odd hardware they have lying around. If you've ever come up to a light and found a pair of vice grips clamped to the carry bar, this is why.
Some operators carry 3 or more pairs of vice grips in different sizes to clamp on to the front or back of a light for weight balance. Different sizes give you different weight options. And you'll probably still have one left over to use for a handle, if you like.

Ratchet Strap – Many people use a ratchet strap to attach the base of their sight to the nose of the lamp rather than using tape. Even if your base has magnets, sometimes a strap is a good idea, particularly with a Telrad on a Stand off base.

1/2" Combination wrench or Gear wrench – this size fits the nuts on the douser plate and the douser handle of a Strong Super Trouper. Because the Douser on a Trouper is the closest control to the lamp and heat, they have a tendency to loosen up over time. Many operators who work with such a lamp on a regular basis keep a ½" wrench in their bag so they can make adjustments to the douser tension or handle once the lamp heats up.

Weight – Many operators carry some kind of weight that they can tie on a light to help balance it so that it stays in place once accessories have been added. (See Balance). Small lengths of chain, shackles of various sizes, T-nuts, C-clamps, Vice Grips, or a water bottle are common weights.

Tie line – It's always a good idea to have some tie line with you, to attach weight to the lamp, to tie off the Chopper handle if you don't want to use it, to safety off sights, stand offs, or any other accessories you have brought up, or to tie errant cables or objects out of your way.

Magnets – some operators like to carry magnets in different sizes, either to hold a sight on the light, or to hold color correction or diffusion on the front of a light, or to hold a cue sheet to a music stand or the side of the light, or to attach a wrench to the light within reach if you have a tricky douser, to name a few uses.

Lint free or microfiber cloth – Cleaning the exposed lens of your lamp, wiping off color, and cleaning booth windows can do wonders for the brightness and sharpness of your lamp. You shouldn't use Windex or any other cleaning solvent on the lens of a lamp. They have coatings that can be smeared or destroyed.

Gaffer's Tape – Usually white, but any color will do in a pinch. This has a bunch of uses for the spot operator, like marking sizes and intensities on the lamp, taping down sights or other accessories, or taping down brads on color frames. You can tape the Chopper handle down so you don't grab it by mistake, or mark it or one of the other handles with a little flag of tape so that the controls are easy to tell apart by feel. You can tape a loose Trombone in place, or mark the spot that it is supposed to be sitting at, or both. You can tape Diffusion or Neutral Density or Color Correction gel on to the front of your light. With white or light colored tape and a marker, you can mark numbers on Boomerang Handles, put little tags on the spot to remind you which way the Iris or Douser works on this lamp, put a little tag on the spot or your window to remind yourself which number spot you are at, or where Stage Left and Stage Right are, or what colors you have in the Boomerang. You can wrap a piece of gaff tape around the carry bar of the light to protect it before you attach a handle or a pair of vice grips to it. You can use it to make an old crappy music stand with your cues on it stay at the proper height. 101 Uses, truly.

Black Sharpie – You can mark all of the stuff mentioned above on your gaff tape. You can mark target positions on a Poster Board above the spot. You can mark up a running order or cue sheet during a tech rehearsal.

Chalk – If you work in a place that uses blackboards above the spots to mark positions, chances are excellent that there will be no chalk when you get up there. Safest to bring your own.

Grease Pencil/China Marker – You can use this to mark gel, either with the color code, or with which frame it needs to go into in the Boomerang. Definitely mark the edge, not the center hot spot of the light. I prefer yellow or white to darker colors.

Another use I have seen – and some venues frown on this, and it is only really helpful if you are in a booth with glass windows, but you can mark colors, or Stage Left and Stage Right, or what number spot you are at, or strategic reminders for cues on the glass of the spot booth window in front of you. Like a fighter pilot's heads up display, you don't have to look away from your target to get information. If you try this, DEFINITELY wipe it off thoroughly when the show is done.

Lubricants – some people carry a can of Lubricant, like Tri-flow or Silicone Spray or even WD-40 with them. It can be helpful, to lubricate a stand that is squeaky or sticky, but many venues really frown on anyone applying any substances to their lights. You should absolutely not lubricate any actual control in or on the light without the express permission of management. It's not a bad idea to check with the folks in charge even about the stand or chair.

Headset – many operators like to carry a personal headset, which is often lighter weight and in better condition than the one you may be issued by the venue. Different intercom systems have different types of jacks and pin configurations for the headset, so you need to make sure that yours has either the right kind of connector for the venues you mostly work in, or an adaptable connector that can work on different systems.

Binoculars – many operators, particularly in a venue with a long throw from the spotlight, like to carry a small pair of binoculars. Besides the popular sport of checking out the audience before the show, they are useful to see what is happening on the stage between cues.

Chapter 15:
Lamp Prep Checklist

Color – You will usually be given color to put in your spot. Sometimes, you are given framed color, sometimes you need to frame it yourself. It is helpful if the number telling you which color is which, is visible once the color is framed, but you don't want it written right in the center hot spot of the light, either. Often, you will be told or given a list of which color goes in which location in the boomerang. #1 is the handle closest to the operator, numbering away from the operator to #6, the handle farthest away from the operator. It's a good idea to write this on the edge of the color as well.

If they leave placement up to you, a general rule of thumb is to have the lighter colors in the handles closest to the operator (and therefore, the lamp and the heat) and the more saturated colors farther away. It's a good idea to write what color ends up where on a post-it or piece of gaff tape to keep close by for reference. Some people take the time to mark the boomerang handles themselves.

If you have frost or diffusion frames, it is often helpful to put them in somewhere easy to remember and easy to grab, like #1 or #6. If you are using "Baggie Frost" – zip top bags cut down to use as diffusion – it is often a good idea to keep it in the #6 position, as far away from the heat as possible. But, changing the distance away from the focal plane changes the quality of the diffusion, and sometimes even the difference between handles in a boomerang can make a difference in the look, so you may need to play around with placement to get the look you want.

Make sure the Boomerang handles all move freely, and colors aren't fouling on each other or on stray brads. Make sure color frames lock into place securely, and release as they should.

You may be given color and/or diffusion to put in a "Drop Frame" which goes in a "Drop Slot" in the center of the light near the focus gate. It's a good idea to trim and tape this so that it slides in and out of the slot guides easily, which often means not having any color hanging over or putting any tape along the long edges, or at least making sure the tape is smooth and even with no breaks or seams.

Most Juliat spotlights have a couple of built in small frames in addition to the Boomerang, generally used for color correction and diffusion.

You may be given a large piece of color (more usually, diffusion or color correction or neutral density) to tape over the front of your lamp, particularly if your lamp doesn't have a Drop Slot.

Strike – once you have color in place, you can usually go ahead and strike your light. (See section on "Firing the Lamp"). If it's early in the day, you may want to wait until closer to showtime to strike the lamp, but you generally need the light on to set focus, aim your sight, and set marks, and you can't really balance the lamp until all your accessories are on and you've set the Trombone, at least. If it's not practical to strike yet, I usually just set the Trombone all the way forward and at least put my sight and accessories on the light so that I can balance and level. Then, I'll come back later, closer to showtime, when I can do the rest.

Focus – Set the focus for the lamp. (See "Parts and Controls"). Some houses have the focus for their lamps set, and don't want individual operators to make any changes. In any permanent venue, this is likely the case. Spots that have been set in place that day for a touring show will probably need their focus adjusted. Most often, the road person in charge of the spotlights will deal with this.

Sometimes, individual operators end up dealing with it, particularly if a loose trombone is sliding around, or has slid all the way to the back, which you almost never really want. The trombone handle should be as far forward as you can get it and still get as large an iris as you need for the show. Once the size is set, the Trombone handle should lock in place (usually by twisting the handle clockwise.) If it won't lock in place, it's a good idea to tape it in place, and if its placement is anything but all the way forward, it's also a good idea to mark the location with a piece of tape. Once the Trombone is set, on many spots, you then need to adjust fine focus with a separate knob to get a sharp edge.

Some smaller spots just have one focus knob, rather than a Trombone and separate Fine Focus. For those spots, you open up your douser to shine your light on stage or a distance equivalent to the stage at approximately Full Body size, then slide or turn the focus adjustment until you get a sharp edge, then lock the adjustment in place.

There are also controls to adjust the centering of the hot spot of the lamp, and to flatten or peak the field of the light, but this is hardly ever anything that a venue or a road show wants an individual operator to mess with. If you feel that your light is way out of whack, you should mention it to the person in charge of the spotlights rather than attempting to deal with it yourself.

Accessories – Put on any sights, standoffs, extra handles, Com belt packs, or anything else that would affect the weight balance of your light. Any accessories that you use should be safetied-off (tied, strapped, or at least taped to your light or your person or a railing or something nearby.)

Balance – (See the "Balance" section). Adjust the level and weight balance of your light so that it will stay in place if you let go of it. Adjust the tightness of your Pan and Tilt locking handles for comfortable operation. You cannot reliably balance until lens focus is done, color is in, and accessories are in place.

Check Controls – Identify your working controls – specifically, your Iris Handle, Chop Handle, and Douser Handle. Figure out where they are and which direction they work in and mark the direction if necessary. You may want to tie or tape off the Chop to make it less likely for you to grab by mistake. Some people like to put a small flag of tape on either the Douser or the Iris to make the two easy to tell apart by feel. Make sure that your controls move freely and stay in place when you let go. Generally, you want to bring any problems to the attention of a supervisor, but in a pinch, like, you're right at showtime, you can sometimes tighten or loosen a Douser handle with a wrench. For one that is loose and floppy and not easily tightened with a wrench, wrap the handle with Gaff tape right at the slot, so the tape slides along the edge of the slot for the handle, to help jam it so it will stay in place when you let go.

Marks – Set marks for your Iris and Douser to help identify sizes and intensities. (See "Sizes and Intensities"). Set marks on a whiteboard or blackboard to identify Center, SL, SR, and Upstage and Downstage Edges, and any specific entrances, set pieces, or other marks you know about. If you are using a sight, set it for the center hotspot of your beam. You may want to set a mark on a board if it's available to give you a backup mark in case you bump your sight. (See "Sights"). You may want to make marks on a railing in front of you to give yourself some ballpark reference points. You may want to mark Boomerang handles. You may want to make marks to remind yourself of SL and SR, or which Number Spotlight you are.

Intercom/Program – You may need to set up your headset and belt pack, or several sets for several spots. (See "Com"). You may need to plug in or turn on show program in a Spotlight Booth, and possibly place monitor speakers near the spots. Good idea to check the system and make sure it works if at all possible before showtime.

You should set up your world – A lot of dedicated spot booths have stuff like chairs and music stands and such permanently in place, but others don't. Depending on the show, the venue, whether you have someone calling cues to you or you are on your own following a cue list or running order or some other document, you may need or want:

- ◆ **A music stand and a light** (which you may need to gel). Many people like to carry a small dimmer that you can put between the stand light and the power source. These are easy to find around the holidays, and often incorporate a dimmer switch in a small extension cord.

- ◆ **A chair.** Some operators prefer to stand, some like to sit. Some people like backs and/or arms on their chairs, some prefer a stool of some kind. Often, space limitations limit or eliminate chair choices. Any chairs used on an open platform or catwalk should be safetied-off.

- **A footrest.** A lot of people like to have a milk crate or some other foot rest when they run a light, particularly if they are sitting. Many booths have these littered around. It is often prudent to bring something up if you aren't sure.

- **A water bottle.** Sometimes, particularly in a booth, you'll have someplace handy to put a bottle of water. Often, it's a good idea to have some kind of water bottle holder or chalk bag that you can secure off somewhere. Doesn't hurt to secure the bottle itself as well. Some venues and shows don't want you to have any food or drink at an open spot position, including water. Some allow water, as long as it's in a bottle with a lid and properly secured.

Chapter 16:
Glossary

Baggie Frost – Frequently, to get a lightweight diffusion look, even the lightest commercial frost is too much on a spotlight. A standard trick to get around this is to use zip-top baggies as your frost gel. Usually, two pieces. Most brands have a slight side to side "grain" to them, and by letting it run side to side on one piece, and then turning the second piece 90 degrees so the grain runs vertically, you cross hatch the grain to make sure that the light spreads evenly. Sometimes, you will want only a single piece. Sometimes, you cut a "donut" – a hole about 3" across – in the middle of one or both pieces. Different people develop different brand preferences, and believe it or not, different brands of baggie and even the Storage and Freezer versions of bags from the same brand actually have different diffusion properties. Gallon Ziploc Storage Bags are the classic for this, but you can experiment.

Balance – Adjusting the weight and level on your spotlight so that it will stay in place when you take your hands off. This should be done after all color and accessories have been added.

Ballyhoo – Moving your light in big circles and/or figure 8's across the stage, or the crowd, or a curtain. Considered festive, it is sometimes called for at Concerts, Circuses, Wrestling matches, and the like.

Bump – Something done instantly, in a 0 count. Like a light switch. You might be asked to "Bump up on the M.C., 100% Full Body, when he gets to Center", or "Bump open to Full Body when he snaps his fingers" or "Standing by to Bump to No Color . . ."

Carry Bar – the long horizontal handles on many spotlights used to steer and move the fixture.

Center Center - the very center of the stage, halfway between the plaster line and the back wall or back of the set, and along the Center line separating Stage Right and Stage Left.

Center Line - an imaginary line running from Upstage to Downstage, splitting the stage in half between Right and Left. Very often, a show will tape down a Center Line to help in placing the set and lighting focus. For some shows, particularly Dance, there may be a physical center line taped or painted on the floor or deck for the show itself.

Chop - The Chopper (also called the shutter, masking shutters, or shaping gate) is a handle on a Spotlight that controls a pair of horizontal shutters that cut off the top and bottom of the light, squaring it off and/or cutting it off of scenery. Some models of Spotlights (Like the Lycian M2) have both a horizontal and a vertical chop. Neither is used very often.

Clock Stage Directions – Dividing a round stage by putting an imaginary clock face on top of it, with the 12 designated by some recognizable landmark like an aisle or an exit sign.

Coat Hanger Sight – a sighting device made from coat hanger wire or similar. One piece gets taped upright to the front of the light, another piece farther back near the operator. Often the rear piece has a loop in the top. Lining these up with the hotspot of your light can make a quick and effective sight.

Color Correction Gel – A gel color meant to correct a fixture's natural color into either a more neutral white, or into a color that more closely blends with the rest of the fixtures in the rig. Often, Xenon lamps, which tend to have a greenish cast, will get a slightly pink gel to compensate. (Rosco 3318 or 3314 for instance). These are sometimes referred to as "minus green" gels. Sometimes, the LD just wants a slightly warmer cast to the light, and they will us a CTO (Color Temperature Orange) gel like Rosco 3408, 3409, or 3410. These are sometimes labeled as 1/8 CTO, ¼ CTO, ½ CTO. Some LD's will put a pale blue color like Lee 201 in a warm lamp to get a cooler color temperature. These are sometimes labeled as CTB (Color Temperature Blue) gels, and may be expressed as 1/8 CTB, ½ CTB, ¼ CTB.

Comets – When you douse a light by dimming the lamp up and down rather than using a physical douser, it takes a few seconds for the filament to completely fade after a fade out. If you move the light before that happens, you can leave a "comet tail" of light behind, which is generally undesirable. This is most commonly a problem when you are using an incandescent light that was not originally intended as a spotlight.

Controls – the devices on your light that directly affect the light. The handles that you typically use in the course of a show – The Douser, Iris, Chopper, and Boomerang. You might also include the Focus controls – the Trombone and/or Fine Focus Knob, which you don't generally manipulate in the course of a show, but do affect the quality of the light.

Cross Shooting – Typically something done with Truss Spots or Side light spots, swapping characters to stay with whichever one is farthest away. Also known as "Zone Defense". Less specifically, any time you are picking up a performer on the opposite side of the stage from where you are located, even from Front of House.

Crossfade – One spotlight fading up as another spotlight (or sometimes the stage light) is fading down.

Cue Sheet – Paper that lists your cues, in order, usually including information about the Target, the Size, the Color, the Intensity, and the Fade Count that is desired for each cue. Sometimes these are built into or written over a Script or a Running Order, which is a list of scenes or events in the show, in order.

Daisy Chain – Plugging several pieces of equipment in from a single feed, with connecting cables going from device to device. Headsets for Spotlight Operators are often "Daisy Chained" together, with the feed for the headsets coming in from the wall to the first belt pack in line, and then out of that pack to the next, and so on down the line.

Daisy Sight - A commercial tube sight that has a small red dot of red light in the center. Powered with a button battery. These are made for Daisy BB Guns, Pellet guns, and the like, and can often be found in either the toy or sporting goods sections of a Big Box store, outdoor store, or online. They come with clips for mounting on a gun, so you have to rig up some kind of mount for it. (The nickname is "Daisy sight", but there are several manufacturers).

Dipstick – The color frame that fits in a slot on top of a spotlight, generally holding Color Correction or Diffusion Gel. Also called a "Drop Frame" or "Slot Frame".

Diffusion – (also called "Frost") a Frosted gel that softens and spreads the edge of your spotlight beam. Rosco 132 or 119 are common examples.

Dorsal Ring – The ring in the upper back of a Full Body Fall Arrest Harness that a Lanyard or Retractable Life Line should be hooked into.

Douser – The control that is used to Dim and Fade Out the light.

Downstage – The area of the stage toward the front of the stage, closest to the audience.

Drop Color – If you are told to Drop Color, it either means to put gel color in your lamp, or to put a dipstick drop frame in if you are doing a show where it comes in and out, or it means to hit your color release lever and go to "Open White" with no color in the boomerang.

Drop Frame - The color frame that fits in a slot on top of a spotlight, generally holding Color Correction or Diffusion Gel. Also called a "Dipstick" or "Slot Frame".

Drop Slot – A slot cut in the top of a spotlight near the focus gate, designed to hold a color frame, generally holding Color Correction or Diffusion Gel. Also called a "Dipstick Slot", since the Color frames themselves are nicknamed "Dipsticks".

English Spotting – An old-fashioned term for using soft edged diffused spots to highlight characters in a more unobtrusive fashion than the classic hard-edged spot. This technique gained wide use and acceptance in American theater with the "invasion" of British shows like "Cats", "Les Miserables" and "Phantom of the Opera" in the 1980's. It is now quite commonplace, particularly in Broadway Theater.

Fall Arrest Harness - a Full Body Harness with a sliding D-ring in the upper back. (Dorsal Ring). To ensure that you have a Legal Fall Arrest Harness that will satisfy OSHA requirements, check the label. It should say that it meets or exceeds ANSI code requirements, and it will cite a specific code number.

Feather the Iris/Ride the Iris – Making small unscripted adjustments of your Iris as a performer moves onstage. Generally opening as they get closer to you, and tightening in as they move farther away, to keep the size consistent. Also, may refer to tightening your iris to stay off the Proscenium, legs, or scenic pieces as your target performer gets close to them, then opening again as they move away.

Fine Focus – the knob on a spotlight that sharpens or fuzzes the edge of the beam of the light.

Flood and Cover – If you are asked to "Flood and Cover", it usually means that there is some kind of emergency, like the main lighting console going down, and they need the spots to open up to flood the stage with light. (This is also sometimes called a "Strip and Cover"). This generally means opening your Iris wide, and often pulling back your Trombone as well to get a wide enough shot to cover the whole stage, then using your Chopper to cut off the top and bottom of your light and frame into the stage. Usually, you would also lock your light in place. If you have a number of spots, you may divide the stage between you.

Front of House – The area of the theater or venue in front of the proscenium or stage. Loosely, any area that is not backstage. More specifically, the area of a venue where the audience is allowed to be. Followspots are often located Front of House.

Frost – (Also called "Diffusion") a Frosted gel that softens and spreads the edge of your spotlight beam.

Full Body – A size designation. As the name implies, it's a shot including the Full Body of the actor, head to feet.

Gate – The focal point of the lamp - the place where the reflector of the lamp forces the individual beams of light to converge. In a spotlight, this is the optimal place for placing controls to shape the light, such as the Iris, the Douser, or the Chop (Shutter).

Ghosting – Either when your douser isn't completely closed, and your light is leaking on the stage, or when an operator intentionally opens their light a crack to see where they are at or check their sight. (Generally frowned upon).
Some operators, who are unsure of their target or their size or whatever will "ghost up", basically fading up VERY slowly so they can make adjustments before they get to their proper intensity. This should be avoided most of the time, although in a tight situation, where you have no sight or it has been knocked off kilter, a slow pickup where you adjust as you go is ultimately better than banging up big and wrong in a hurry. It's more commonly done in Rock and Roll type shows where such pickups are not as obvious.

Half Body – A size. Basically, the same as a Waist shot. Sometimes, a half body means including a specific piece of costume, like a suit coat, or even including the performer's hands at his side, although you would usually want a larger size for that.
Head – the actual luminaire of the spotlight. The main unit that houses the lamp and controls. The Head sets into the Yoke, which sets into the Base or a pipe mount or an overhead fitting.

Head Shot – Sized to pick up just a performer's head. Very often, this is as small as the Iris will go. Usually, a head shot includes any hat or headdress that a performer may be wearing.

Hollywood – A kind of old-fashioned technique where a spot or spots sweep back and forth across a line of performers, often during bows. I believe the nickname comes from the fact that the bit is supposed to sort of simulate the look of old Hollywood Searchlights at a big event.

Home Color – sometimes, a caller will tell you that a specific color frame or color combination is your "Home Color". It can simplify the call if whoever is calling cues for the spots can just periodically tell everyone to go to their "Home Color".

Home Positions – sometimes, a caller will tell you that a person or location is your "Home Position". It can simplify the call if whoever is calling cues for the spots can just periodically tell everyone to go to their "Home Positions".

Horizontal Lifeline – A safety line run across the top of a truss or roof beam that you can clip the lanyard from your Fall Arrest Harness into.

Hot Spot – The center of your beam of light. The brightest "hottest" part of the light. Some venues will set the hot spot of the spotlights slightly above the actual center of the beam, to aid in getting the best light on the performer's face. Depending on how your lamp has been focused, the "hot spot" of the light may be more or less difficult to see. Ideally, the light is focused to have a flat, even field of light, but some technicians will deliberately leave the field a bit "peaked" to give you an identifiable brighter, hotter, center. This can help your brightness, particularly in smaller sizes. Any adjustment of the field focus on a lamp should be left to the people who maintain the lights for the building.

House Left/Right – The Left or Right side of the stage as viewed from the house. Spot callers rarely use "House" directions. Usually, when they refer to Left and Right, they mean Stage Left and Stage Right, the sides of the stage as viewed from the performer's perspective, facing the audience, even if you are out front.

HMI Lamp – HMI stands for Hydrargyrum medium-arc iodide. It is the trademark name of Osram's brand of metal-halide gas discharge medium arc-length lamps. Often found in Small to Mid-Size Followspots, HMI fixtures tend to have a warmer color temperature than Xenon lamps. Like all Arc Lamps, they must be powered through a ballast, and the fixture must have a mechanical douser to dim them rather than being able to dim the lamp itself.

Intensity – how bright or dim your light is. Most spot callers and cue sheets designate intensities as percentages of Full, or 100% Intensity.

Iris – The control that is used to make the beam of your light larger and smaller. The Trombone, which controls the placement of the front lens of the lamp, will also affect what sizes your spot is able to achieve. Once the Trombone has been set, the Iris will control your size during the show.

Knee Shot – A size designation. As the name implies, lighting a performer from the Knees up.

Knurled Knob – The fine focus control on a Strong Super Trouper

Lanyard – a strap that you hook to your harness to connect to an anchor point. For Fall Arrest purposes, you must connect it to the Dorsal Ring of your Fall Arrest Harness to clip off to a lifeline or anchor point. Many lanyards come with shock absorbers built in. A proper Lanyard should be no more than 6' long, including any shock absorber that it may have.
Leveling Feet – Feet on a spotlight base that can screw up or down to help level the fixture.

Live Swing – Moving your light from one place or character to another with the light on. This is sometimes done intentionally, for effect, swinging up to an entrance, for instance, or to a performer for dramatic effect.

Sometimes, though, this happens unintentionally, either when an operator allows their target to walk out of their light and then swings to catch up or realizes that they are in the wrong place or on the wrong character and does a panicked swing to the right location. This is very bad unprofessional behavior. You need to resist your first panicked reaction. If you have lost your character, or you are in the wrong place for whatever reason, you should fade out, find your target, and fade in again. Done smoothly, most of the audience will never notice. Sometimes, the spot caller won't even notice.

A Live Swing is sometimes referred to as a "Prison Break", particularly if it looks like the light is sweeping around searching for its target like an old-fashioned prison movie.

Manyard – a Lanyard with a shock absorber integrated into it.

Master Card – When two or more performers stand side by side, and two spots cover with a slight overlap, making their lights look like a Master Card logo. Can be used as a verb "Can you two spread out and Master Card that group?"

Neutral Density Gel – This is a greyish gel used to reduce intensity in a fixture without changing the color temperature of the lamp. Often used in film. They come in a variety of darkness, sometimes expressed as .3,.6, or .9 ND. All the major manufacturers make them. Examples would be Lee 209, 210 & 211, or GAM 1514, 1515, 1516). Sometimes, if you have a spotlight that is very bright for the application you are using it in, an LD will decide to put Neutral Density gel in the drop slot or taped to the front of the spot to bring the overall level down, either because you are doing a dark show, or to balance two spots that have very different intensities.

Offstage – any area of the stage that is out of the audience's view. Sometimes used as a direction, meaning away from center and toward the wings. "Pan your light a little more offstage and include that handbasket"

Onstage – the area of the stage in the audience's view. Sometimes used as a direction, meaning towards center from wherever you are now. "Cheat your light a little more onstage to get off that Proscenium wall"

Open White – No color at all in the spotlight. If you are asked to go to "Open White", they want you to release all the color frames from your boomerang.

Overlay – Some LD's like to put two spots on a performer for a specific look – often in a slow ballad where the performer is still. Typically, one spot will be on the performer in either a full body shot or in a ¾ shot covering everything except the performer's face – highlighting a dress, for example. Usually this person is in some kind of strong saturated color. Then, the other spot picks up the performer's head, or head and shoulders, or even head to waist in a contrasting color. Usually something lighter and more flattering for the face.

Pan – Move side to side

Perfect Pick-Up – A sight. A commercial version of the home-made coat hanger sight. It attaches to your lamp with a magnet. There is a standoff to hold it away from a light, and then a thin rod that folds out horizontal to the lamp with a small ring on the front end and a larger ring on the back end that you align with the hot spot of your lamp and lock in place. It travels folded up in a little tube.

Pick-Up – term used for bringing your light up on a performer. "Standby to pick-up the Bass Player".

Pin Spot – The smallest spot your Iris will allow. Used to pick up just a performer's face, or some tiny object or spot on the stage.

Porky Pig – Irising in to a headshot in a big obvious way, usually with a hard edge. (Like the end of the old Looney Tunes cartoons.) Usually followed by a bump out. With a spot that allows you to Iris completely out, like many of the Juliats, you may just Iris out. Sometimes it's all one move, irising right down and out, although it's more likely, if they're calling it a Porky Pig, that you would iris in to a head shot, then wait for a line or a wink or some other cue, or a cue from a caller, and then either continue the iris out or bump out with a douser. Sometimes you are asked to fade down in intensity as you iris in.

Pressure Switch – a sensor inside the lamp house of some units which can sense the air pressure and can cut the lamp off if the pressure drops because the airflow is restricted or the housing around the lamp comes loose. May also refer to a switch that senses whether a pin is physically depressed indicating that the lid of the lamp house or fixture is in place.

Prison Break – When a spotlight is sweeping across the stage, looking for their performer, or chasing after a performer who has walked out of their light. Unless it's being done for intentional effect, it's generally a huge no-no, and makes most LD's very upset. (See Live Swing).

Quarter Line – A line halfway between the Center Line and the edge of the stage. (So, you will have a "Quarter Line Left" and a "Quarter Line Right"). Ballet companies usually mark the Quarter Lines on a stage, and sometimes they even put tiny lighted indicators at Quarter lines and Center line to help Dancers orient themselves during a performance. Some spot callers, particularly in Ballet, will use the term to tell you where a pickup is or will be.

Retractable Lifeline – Also commonly called a Yo-yo or a Teardrop. This is a safety line hung from overhead that drops down to be clipped in to the Dorsal Ring of your Fall Arrest Harness with a special hook. It acts like a seat belt in your car – it unspools and retracts as you move, but any sudden move, like a fall, will cause it to jerk up short and hold you in place. <u>THESE ARE DESIGNED TO BE HOOKED DIRECTLY TO THE D-RING OF YOUR HARNESS, NOT TO A LANYARD OR MANYARD.</u>

Ride the Iris/Feather the Iris – Making small unscripted adjustments of your Iris as a performer moves onstage. Generally opening as they get closer to you, and tightening in as they move farther away, to keep the size consistent. Also, may refer to tightening your iris to stay off the Proscenium, legs, or scenic pieces as your target performer gets close to them, then opening again as they move away.

Roll Color – Changing from one color or colors to another live, in audience view. Sometimes they will want you to roll one color out and the other color in slowly, which can be a tricky maneuver for the operator, particularly if you are also following a moving target at the time. Sometimes, they just want to bump from one color to another, which is much easier to achieve.

Running Order - a list of scenes or events in the show, in order. Sometimes you will be given one of these instead of or in addition to a Cue Sheet.

Sight – A device that an operator attaches to their spotlight to aid in hitting an exact point for a pickup. There are many types, some home-made and some commercial.

Shock Absorber – Attached or built into a Lanyard for Fall Arrest, to slow and ease the shock of a fall. Also called a Zorber, Zipper, or Screamer. There are a couple of different styles of shock absorber, the simplest of which is a bungee style that has elastic to help take your weight at the bottom of a fall. More common is a webbing strap that has been loosely sewn together in back and forth folds, which release as your weight hits, one seam at a time, slowing your fall.

Shutter – Another name for the Chop control. (See Chop). Some models of Spotlights (Like the Lycian M2) have both horizontal and vertical shutters. Neither is used very often.

Slide – Moving from one character to another live. Similar to a swap, except that you are not exchanging characters with another spot. Some callers just say swap for this as well.

Slot Frame – The color frame that fits in a slot on top of a spotlight, generally holding Color Correction or Diffusion Gel. Also called a "Drop Frame" or "Dipstick".

Spot Dot – A commercial tube sight that has a small red dot of red light in the center. This sight is very small and portable. Powered with a button battery. Comes with a mount/stand-off.

Spot Size Control Knob – Commonly called the Trombone, which controls the placement of the forward lens of the lamp, and therefore the size range that the spot can achieve. (See Trombone).

Stage Left/Right – Stage Left is the left side of the stage from the performer's point of view – that is, standing on stage looking out at the audience. Stage Right is the right side from that point of view. Even if you are facing the other way, as spotlight operators usually are, Stage Left and Stage Right do not change. They remain Left and Right from the performer's perspective.

Strip and Cover – If you are asked to "Strip and Cover", it usually means that there is some kind of emergency, like the main lighting console going down, and they need the spots to open up to flood the stage with light. (This is also sometimes called a "Flood and Cover"). This generally means dropping your color ("Strip"), opening your Iris wide, and often pulling back your Trombone as well to get a wide enough shot to cover the whole stage, then using your Chopper to cut off the top and bottom of your light and frame into the stage. Usually, you would also lock your light in place. If you have a number of spots, you may divide the stage between you.

Swap – Sliding your light from one performer to another live. Usually done when two characters are in close proximity. (And sometimes called a "Proximity Swap"). Very often, done in conjunction with another spot, who is "swapping" to the character you have just left – you exchange targets. This is very common with Side or Truss spots, continually swapping to stay with whichever performer is facing you or is farthest away. If you are left to make such swaps on your own, this is often called "Cross Shooting" or "Zone Defense".

Telrad – A commercial Spotlight sight, originally made for Telescopes. (Full name – Telrad Reflex Sight). It features a fairly large window with a lit red Bulls-eye, which can be dimmed to various stages of brightness. It has little knobs on the back to align the bulls-eye with the Hot Spot of your lamp. Telrads come with a separate base. Stand offs are sold separately.

Three Quarter Body – A size roughly analogous to a Knee shot, although sometimes 3/4 means somewhere in between a Waist and a Knee shot, including a performer's hands at his side and/or the bottom of a coat or other costume piece.

Throw – the distance between the light and the target, or the light and the stage.

Tilt – the Up and Down motion of the light.

Trombone – This knob controls the placement of the front lens of a spotlight, changing the focal length, which affects how big a spot can be projected from a given throw distance. The farther forward on the lamp that the Trombone is set, the longer the focal length, and therefore, the smallest, brightest spot available. Sometimes the Trombone needs to be set farther back to allow for the sizes needed for a particular show or moment in a show. On a light without a separate fine focus adjustment, the Trombone should be set where it gives you the cleanest sharpest edge. On many lights, after the Trombone is set, fine focus is achieved with a separate knob, and size changes throughout the show are usually achieved with the Iris control.

Tube Sight – A popular home-made sight, particularly helpful for smaller lamps and shorter throw distances. You take a small tube, often PVC or conduit, about 3" – 4" long, and stand it off from your light with a small length of wire or plumber's strap. Usually, it attaches to your light with either a magnet or just Gaff tape. You align the tube so you can look through it at the center hot spot of your light. It is a good idea, particularly for a truss spot, to "safety" it off with a piece of tie line as well.

Two Shot – A term borrowed from Film and TV. Picking up two people in the same spotlight. May be adapted to "Three shot" and so on. Sometimes called a "Cover Two".

Upstage – towards the back wall, away from the audience.

Waist Shot – A spot sized to include everything from the Waist up on a performer.

Xenon Lamp – An arc lamp used in large Spotlights (and some projectors) that contains gas – primarily Xenon – inside the lamp envelope. Xenon lamps are powerful and the light they emit tends to be cool and slightly greenish in color compared to most incandescent stage fixtures, which helps to pop a performer out of the stage picture. Like all Arc Lamps, they must be powered through a ballast, and the fixture must have a mechanical douser to dim them rather than being able to dim the lamp itself. Xenon lamps are pressurized and very volatile, especially when hot, and can explode if they or the fixture that they are in are hit or jarred suddenly. They should only be handled by trained professionals with appropriate safety gear.

Yo – Yo – A nickname for a Retractable Life Line. (See Retractable Life Line).

Yoke – the Y shaped frame that holds the spotlight head. It has a swivel built in to allow the unit to pan and has a pipe that either sets into a base on the floor, a coupling on a pipe, or slides up into an overhead fitting. Tilt and Pan controls are usually located on the yoke. Most stands have a way to set the yoke at different heights.

Zone Defense – Sometimes a caller will tell you to stay with whichever performer is on your side of the stage, swapping off with another spot or spots as performers change places. More usually, this is used for side or Truss spots, and you are staying with whichever performer of a pair is facing you, or farthest away from you, while a spot on the opposite side is doing the same, swapping from performer to performer as they change places. This is also called "Cross Shooting".

www.ingramcontent.com/pod-product-compliance
Lightning Source LLC
LaVergne TN
LVHW021545080426
835509LV00019B/2850